The
HEALTHY
Cookbook
for TEENS

The HEALTHY Cookbook for TEENS

100 FAST & EASY DELICIOUS RECIPES

NOAH MICHAUD

Photography by Thomas J. Story

ROCKRIDGE
PRESS

Interior and Cover Designer: Antonio Valverde
Art Producer: Sue Smith
Editor: Eliza Kirby
Production Editor: Mia Moran

Photography © 2019 Thomas J. Story
Food styling by Karen Shinto
Author photo courtesy of © Ben Michaud

ISBN: Print 978-1-64152-864-1 | eBook 978-1-64152-865-8

R0

To all who have sat at my table
whom I've had the pleasure to feed.
Thanks for fueling my culinary fire
from day one onward.

This book is for you.

Contents

Introduction

Hey there! Chances are, if you've come across this book, you're a teen who wants to learn to cook. Or someone you know—a parent, grandparent, friend, or more-than-friend—wants you to learn to cook. Or maybe you've got some experience in the kitchen and you want to check out this book to further your learning. Regardless of how you ended up here, I'm glad you did. Cooking is fun and functional. It pleases the eyes, the stomach, and the spirit all at once! And, when done well, it's healthy.

Healthy. Often, when we hear the word, "healthy," we also think of things like "diet" and "restrictions" and "expensive." Granted, "healthy" sometimes gives us a great feeling—because we know that eating healthily feels good—but it can also be confusing. As kids, we might have cringed at the thought of "secretly healthy" food. But even after we've outgrown our distaste for things green and leafy, many of us are left with questions. *How hard is healthy cooking? How many substitutions do I need to remember—because healthy food depends on them, right? How can anything that's healthy taste good? When's cheat day? And, sure, there are all sorts of pre-made healthy stuff at the store, but how do I make my own food healthy?*

I wrote this book for people just like you to help clear up the confusion around how to cook food that tastes amazing *and* is generally good for you. The recipes in this book provide a foundation for healthy home cooking that builds upon basic techniques and classics and incorporates a taste of more advanced cooking methods as you gain some culinary confidence. Creativity is one of the best parts of cooking—healthy cooking included.

Before I get ahead of myself, though, I should introduce myself. I'm Noah. Nice to meet you. I've spent a while refining the recipes in *The Healthy Cookbook for Teens* so they are quick and easy, and use simple ingredients—but are also impressive—with teens like you and me in mind. (Actually, by the time you're reading these words I'll be twenty, but I started cooking in my tweens.) Point is,

I've packed this book with all sorts of tips, tricks, and tales to help you practice and perfect your kitchen chops.

Even if you've never cooked before, this book will give you the skills you need to start making tasty meals right away. I remember how satisfying it was the first time I cooked something delicious on my own. I took my time (I was no knife skills ninja) but the payoff from the patience and perseverance—the sense of achievement, my family's reactions, and, of course, tasting the delicious results myself—made it something I *definitely* wanted to do again.

By consulting this book, I hope that you, too, will create your own culinary memories—that you will not only learn the foundations of cooking as a teen but also find yourself well on your way to creating some of your own wonderful, wholesome dishes. I have complete confidence in you. Think of all the delicious rewards that await you at your table!

So, are you in? Great.

Let's get cooking!

1
GET COOKING!

Welcome!

Before you start cooking from *The Healthy Cookbook for Teens*, I want to introduce some principles of healthy cooking as well as the tasks and tools of the kitchen. Feel free to turn back to this chapter as you cook; it contains everything you'll need to know to successfully prepare the recipes in the book.

Healthy Cooking

As I touched on in the introduction, the term "healthy cooking" can be confusing. What exactly is it? More importantly, how does this book define it?

The healthiest cooking is sustainable, meaning it's clean, straightforward, interesting, and replicable. Healthy cooking is easy to stick to because the qualifications are simple. Most recipes in this book are "healthy" in that they primarily rely on whole food (unprocessed) ingredients, which contain more of their natural fiber, vitamins, and minerals.

What does a mostly whole foods approach mean? For one, cooking from whole ingredients sidesteps the majority of preservatives and additives in processed ingredients. Fresh ingredients look and taste better. For another, it means the cook controls the recipe much more precisely.

Finally, and perhaps unexpectedly, defining "healthy cooking" with a whole foods approach makes healthy eating a bit more flexible. The key with more classically "unhealthy" foods, like butter, is to use them in moderation. Balancing our diet by cooking and eating whole foods also comes with myriad health benefits, such as lower risks of disease, but those may already be familiar to you. (See Resources on page 196 for more information.)

The whole foods approach means mainly cooking with fresh produce and unrefined ingredients (think whole grains). Frozen and canned ingredients are okay if they are all natural and low on processing and added sugars. When using fresh produce, it's important to know what chemicals, if any, the foods have been treated with while growing or harvesting. The Dirty Dozen and the Clean Fifteen™ lists (see page 195), released annually by the Environmental Working Group (EWG), are your guide to knowing whether to buy conventional products or organic varieties of certain produce. Along with forgoing preservatives and other additives, we'd prefer to consume as few pesticides as possible. Therefore, it's best to wash your fruits, veggies, and herbs well before using, just for good measure.

And although it is certainly no requirement of healthy cooking or the whole foods approach, I find it beneficial (and more interesting) to cook and eat with the seasons. In other words, buy and cook different produce throughout the year according to when it's naturally grown and harvested—it will taste and look its best during its season. In many cases, though not always, the best seasonal produce is found at local vendors or farmers' markets. When produce is in season locally, you can usually find it in supermarkets, too, coming from a close-by supplier. By the way, closer often means cheaper, so eating seasonally is one way to make eating healthier more affordable.

I tend to think each season has its own palette of flavors and ingredients:

- **SPRING:** bright, grassy, green, and fresh; think of vegetables such as asparagus and peas.
- **SUMMER:** also bright and fresh; berries, tomatoes, watermelon, and summer squash come to mind.
- **AUTUMN:** earthy ingredients, warm spices, and root vegetables; apples, pumpkins, corn, carrots, and mushrooms, for instance.
- **WINTER:** similar to autumn, earthy and hearty; lots of root vegetables such as beets and winter squash.

You may notice some overlap here, or that the local produce available near you follows a slightly different pattern. That's fine! You might even be eating seasonally already without realizing it. Ultimately, eating with the seasons helps you make the best tasting, most nutritious food using ingredients at their prime, and it keeps you aware of where your food comes from (if you're not sure what's in season near you, there are many seasonal food guides online).

Essentially, healthy cooking through a mostly whole foods approach isn't very different from "normal" cooking. It's simply more mindful cooking and eating. It's knowing what you're cooking and when to cook with it to get the best result. It's being more aware of what goes into a recipe and making a few easy modifications when necessary to keep everything balanced nutritionally. It's really not too complicated.

If you've never cooked before or are just starting out, healthy cooking is a wonderful place to start. If you are already somewhat experienced in the kitchen but haven't considered this approach, I encourage you to make these ideas central to your cooking.

Now for a crash course in the fundamental tools and techniques of the culinary arts.

The Basics

Great cooking revolves around mastering basic techniques. Without understanding the basic methods, we can't execute them properly and, when the time comes, adapt them! I've organized this list into two categories: *knife skills* and *preparations*.

Knife Skills

HOLDING A KNIFE: Grasp the handle with the thumb and forefinger. Wrap the other fingers around it.

GUIDING HAND POSITION: Cup your other hand like a claw, bringing your wrist up, and tucking your fingers and thumb back to prevent cuts.

CHOP: Cutting something roughly into pieces of about the same size, disregarding shape; often accomplished in a rocking, crossing motion with the knife.

- *Dice:* Cutting something into pieces of uniform size and shape, often square; small, medium, and large dice are most common. Many recipes call for diced onion, for example.

- *Mince:* Chopping or dicing something into such small pieces they almost dissolve in the final dish. We often mince pungent ingredients such as garlic and shallots when we don't want the pieces to be detectable.

Continued on next page

Continued from previous page

SLICE: Cutting something into cross sections; to cut one way as opposed to two (chop or dice).

- ***Shave:*** Slicing something quite thin with a vegetable peeler, a mandoline, or a knife. Buffalo Chicken Grilled Cheese (page 77), for example, features shaved carrot and celery.

The following terms are less important, but the techniques are used throughout the book:

- To "cut into medium and small, thin matchsticks," respectively, is to *batonnet* and *julienne*. Often, a true julienne is more for aesthetics, whereas a rougher julienne (i.e., not perfect cuts) is more practical.

- Rolling stacked leaves into a cigar shape and slicing across them to make "thin ribbons" is to *chiffonade* (a French term). Chiffonade is used with leafy herbs and vegetables such as basil and lettuces.

Preparations

BAKE: This usually entails cooking over lesser surface area for longer periods of time and often uses the steam generated during the cooking process to help cook the food from the inside out.

ROAST: To cook at high heat over a large surface area to create a brown, dry crust on food. I often roast vegetables.

- *Broil:* Cooking at very high heat close to a heating element to encourage rapid cooking, browning, toasting, or melting.

TOAST: To crisp breads or the surfaces of food to form a crust; alternatively, to lightly brown in a pan to enhance flavor.

BOIL: To cook foods submerged in liquids at temperatures above 200°F (above 212°F, and you've got a *rapid, rolling boil*).

- *Blanch:* Boiling food briefly (from just seconds up to 1 to 2 minutes) and quickly halting the cooking completely by shocking the food in ice water. I blanch many green vegetables.

- *Steam*: To cook using contained steam from a liquid.

SIMMER: This method of wet cooking happens over a longer period of time at lower temperatures (think small bubbles).

- *Braise:* To simmer food after quickly browning it, at least partially submerged in liquid after it's been seared. This method is often used to prepare stews, to tenderize tougher cuts of meat, and to cook some vegetables.

- *Poach:* To cook gently and slowly in a hot, often flavorful liquid. Poaching liquids usually do not bubble as much as simmering liquids. Poached eggs are a common example, but also poached fruit.

Continued on next page

Continued from previous page

Sauté: To cook quickly in a pan with a little fat over medium high heat, moving the food often.

- *Sweat:* To cook vegetables in a pan so they become tender while developing little color, often used in preparing soups and sauces.

- *Panfry:* To cook entirely in a pan, using more fat and more moderate heat than sautéing. (Often, I finish a dish by panfrying it in the oven.)

- *Sear:* To develop a brown crust on food over very high heat, quickly and with very little fat.

- *Caramelize:* To brown the natural or added sugars found in food; this can be done quickly, but is more often done over an extended period of time to minimize burning. You'll use this method with French Onion Quiche (page 139).

GRILL: To cook quickly, with little fat, over an oiled and hot grate.

PURÉE: This is often done in a blender or food processor to transform solid ingredients into a uniform liquid (of any thickness).

MARINATE: To submerge a food in a flavored mixture of fat, acid, and seasonings to tenderize and flavor it.

I think that just about covers all techniques needed for the recipes in this book.

The Tools

Every chef needs their arsenal of tools to make the process as efficient as possible. Here are my equipment go-tos, categorized into must-haves and nice-to-haves for starting out. You might already have many of these items and can certainly find more advanced tools as your skills develop!

Must-Haves

- ☑ **Blender:** for blending and puréeing
- ☑ **Can opener**
- ☑ **Colander:** for straining large items
- ☑ **Cookware:**
  - *for baking:* sheet pan, muffin tin, and baking dishes
  - *for cooking:* saucepan, skillet or sauté pan, and Dutch oven or soup pot with lid
- ☑ **Cutting boards**
- ☑ **Instant-read thermometer:** so we don't serve improperly cooked food
- ☑ **Knives:** Choose quality knives you are comfortable holding, and take care of them—they will serve you long and well!
  - *chef's knife (all-purpose)*
  - *paring knife (for smaller tasks)*
  - *serrated knife (for bread and tomatoes)*

Continued on next page

Continued from previous page

- ☑ **Measuring:** cups—liquid and solid—and spoons
- ☑ **Mixing bowls:** one small, one medium, one large
- ☑ **Potholders, oven mitts, and/or kitchen towels:** for kitchen safety
- ☑ **Spatulas**
- ☑ **Whisk:** for, well, whisking and whipping
- ☑ **Wooden spoons:** slotted and solid, for all your stirring needs

Nice-to-Haves

- ☑ **Box grater:** for grating cheeses and vegetables
- ☑ **Food processor:** a versatile tool for grating, slicing, blending, and puréeing quicker than a blender
- ☑ **Grill or grill pan**
- ☑ **Handheld rasp (Microplane):** for grating cheese, aromatics, and spices, and for zesting citrus
- ☑ **Kitchen shears:** for anything and everything dealing with trimming food and food packaging (wash them often)
- ☑ **Ladle:** for serving soups, stews, and sauces
- ☑ **Spring-loaded tongs:** a mainstay for turning, grabbing, and serving
- ☑ **Spring-loaded scoop:** for baking, portioning, and ice cream!
- ☑ **Vegetable peeler:** for peeling, but also for shaving fruits, vegetables, cheeses, and chocolate

A Quick Note
on Kitchen Safety

Cuts, burns, and bruises—*oh my*! The kitchen is a dangerous place when not approached with your full attention. That said, if you use proper technique for holding a knife, handle hot items with appropriate protection, and refrain from doing anything too risky or dangerous without fully understanding how to do it safely, the kitchen is not something to fear. I can say firsthand that injuries do occur in the kitchen. It is a part of the process—accidents happen. However, following proper precautions will lessen your chances of a serious injury. This chapter, and notes in the recipes, will give you that knowledge.

In addition, follow proper food-safety protocols. Store food in your refrigerator at 40°F and freezer at 0°F. Keep raw and cooked foods separate, especially meat and seafood. And wash your hands frequently while cooking and especially after handling raw meat, fish, poultry, seafood, or eggs.

About the Recipes

The recipes in this book have been designed with the principles of healthy cooking in mind. Most recipes take no more than 45 minutes of active cooking time, feature about 10 ingredients or fewer (excluding water, salt, pepper, and a few homemade seasoning blends and garnishes), and are flavorful and delicious.

Some recipes fit well into patterns of seasonal eating. For instance, Twice-Baked Sweet Potatoes (page 122) are perfect for chilly fall or winter nights, whereas Golden Gazpacho (page 56), a chilled soup, makes a wonderful summer afternoon lunch.

This book features 100 recipes, spanning breakfasts, salads, soups, main dishes for one, dishes for group occasions, side dishes, snacks, drinks, and desserts. Many are classic favorites with a healthy or flavorful twist. Others are a little more adventurous. Almost all the ingredients needed should be available at your local grocery store; the remaining few can be found at a health foods market such as Whole Foods or The Fresh Market. Healthy cooking is most useful when it's accessible!

Each recipe falls into one or more of the following categories. Use these labels to tell at a glance if a recipe is what you're looking to make for a particular meal:

🔖 *Dairy-Free*	🔖 *Grain-Free*
☑ *Extra Quick:*	🔖 *Nut-Free*
30 minutes or under!	🔖 *Vegan*
🔖 *Gluten-Free*	🔖 *Vegetarian*

The majority of these recipes also come with tips on ingredients or their preparations. I offer tidbits, facts, and more specific instructions for special ingredients. This is just further proof that everything you need to succeed at healthy, whole food cooking is contained in this book. You can do this!

Finally, in the back of the book, in addition to the Dirty Dozen and the Clean Fifteen™ charts (see page 195), you'll find further Resources (see page 196) on healthy eating and cooking to inspire you and help you continue your culinary odyssey.

You're all set now.

Good luck, and bon appétit!

2

BREAKFASTS

Nut-Free
Vegetarian

Active time:
10 minutes

Total time:
15 minutes

Cooking tip
The blackberries should start sizzling as soon as they hit the pan. If you think the pan is getting too hot, remove it from the heat to prevent burning.

Technique tip
Zesting citrus is a common technique in many recipes (and especially in this book). To zest citrus is to remove the surface of its outer peel; run the fruit along a grater, but make sure to rotate the fruit to minimize the amount of bitter pith in your zest.

Ingredient tip
You can find crystallized ginger in the dried fruit and nuts section of your grocery store or specialty market such as Whole Foods, or you can order it online.

Blackberry Toast
with Lemon Ginger Ricotta

☑ **Extra Quick** ★ **Serves 2**

This toast is sure to wake you up with its bright flavors of blackberry, lemon, and ginger. Slightly sweet ricotta and honey mellow the sharp notes for one creamy and energizing bite!

1 ½ teaspoons honey, plus more for drizzling

Heaping ½ cup fresh blackberries

1 cup ricotta

Grated zest of 1 lemon

½ teaspoon ground ginger

¼ teaspoon kosher salt

2 thick slices multigrain bread, toasted

Crystallized ginger, chopped, for topping (optional)

1 In a small pan over high heat, pour the honey in an even layer. Immediately add the blackberries—seek out that loud sizzle! Toss the berries to coat them in the honey and cook for no more than 1 minute. Remove the pan from the heat and set aside on a heatproof surface to cool.

2 In a small bowl, stir together the ricotta, lemon zest, ground ginger, and salt.

3 Assemble the toast: Place the toast slices on a work surface and spread the ricotta mixture evenly over them. Top each with half the blistered blackberries, a drizzle of honey, and a sprinkle of crystallized ginger (if using).

Avocado Toast
with Golden Raisins and Goat Cheese

☑ *Extra Quick* ★ *Serves 2*

No healthy cookbook would be complete without a recipe for avocado toast. Tangy goat cheese, vinegar, golden raisins, and sunflower seeds dress up the typical toast and complement the rich avocado. A great avo-toast is a lesson in simplicity and balance.

¼ cup golden raisins

1 cup warm water

2 tablespoons sunflower seeds

1 avocado, halved and pitted (see tip)

2 slices multigrain bread, toasted

¼ cup goat cheese, crumbled

¾ teaspoon white wine vinegar, or white balsamic vinegar

Kosher salt

Freshly ground black pepper

1 In a small bowl, combine the raisins and warm water to rehydrate while you toast the seeds.

2 In a small dry pan over medium heat, toast the sunflower seeds for 5 minutes, stirring often. Transfer the seeds to a small bowl so they don't continue to cook and burn.

3 With a spoon, scoop the avocado halves out of their skins. Thinly slice the flesh and place half the avocado on each piece of toast. Smash the slices with a fork to create a textured avocado spread.

4 Drain the raisins.

5 Evenly sprinkle the goat cheese, plumped raisins, and sunflower seeds over the avocado.

6 Drizzle the toppings with vinegar. Season with salt and pepper.

Nut-Free

Vegetarian

Active time:
10 minutes

Total time:
15 minutes

Ingredient tip

To pit an avocado, halve it by carefully using a knife to cut around the avocado lengthwise—make a cut in the center that follows the circumference of the fruit. Twist the two halves apart. Remove the pit by firmly tapping the seed with the knife blade. Twist the knife to remove the pit. Pinch the knife around the pit to release it. You can also use a spoon to scoop out the pit.

Gluten-Free
Vegetarian

Active time:
5 minutes

Total time:
10 minutes

Ingredient tip
You can find acai in the frozen fruit section of your grocery store or specialty ingredient store. Acai is also sold as a powder; replace the frozen pulp with 1 scoop of powder in this recipe.

Blueberry-Acai Bowl

☑ **Extra Quick** ★ **Serves 1**

A staple breakfast from Brazil, acai smoothie bowls have gained a lot of traction in the United States over the past few years. It's easy to see why—they are simple, quick, nutritious, and refreshing, not to mention beautiful to look at. Blueberry and acai is a go-to combination that's loaded with healthy antioxidants and blends into a gorgeous violet color.

1 cup frozen blueberries

1 banana, sliced and frozen

1 (3.5-ounce) pouch frozen acai pulp

Freshly squeezed lemon juice (from a small piece of lemon)

1 banana, cut into rounds

Coconut chips, or unsweetened shredded coconut, for garnish

Cranberry, Chocolate, and Hazelnut Granola (page 26), or all-natural store-bought granola, for garnish (optional)

Low-fat Greek yogurt, or coconut yogurt, for garnish (optional)

1   In a blender, combine the frozen blueberries, frozen banana, acai pulp, and lemon juice. Purée until smooth and thick, no more than 3 minutes. Pour the fruit purée into a deep bowl.

2   Top with the banana rounds and garnish with coconut chips, granola, and yogurt (if using).

Herbed Scrambled Eggs

☑ *Extra Quick* ⋆ *Serves 2*

Fluffy and luscious, these scrambled eggs easily elevate everyday breakfast from plain to perfection. Parsley, thyme, and chives provide a fresh green bite. Serve with a piece of multigrain toast.

3 tablespoons unsalted butter

4 large eggs, room temperature

1 teaspoon kosher salt

1 teaspoon chopped fresh flat-leaf parsley

1 teaspoon chopped fresh chives

1 teaspoon chopped fresh thyme leaves

⅛ teaspoon freshly ground black pepper

1. In a medium glass bowl, microwave the butter until just melted (the fat should not separate from the milk solids), no more than 1 minute. Set aside to cool for 2 minutes.
2. Add the eggs to the melted butter and whisk until well combined and evenly lemon-yellow throughout.
3. In a small skillet or saucepan over medium-low heat, cook the butter and egg mixture for 5 to 6 minutes, continuously agitating the mixture with a wooden spoon or heatproof spatula, scraping from one edge of the pan, through the center, and to the other edge of the pan to form small egg curds. You should hear a very quiet sizzle from the pan.
4. When little liquid egg remains, but *not* when the pan is completely dry, season the eggs with salt, parsley, chives, thyme, and pepper. Remove the skillet from the heat, stir to mix well, and serve.

Gluten-Free

Grain-Free

Nut-Free

Vegetarian

Active time:
8 minutes

Total time:
10 minutes

Cooking tip
Stop cooking your eggs slightly before you think you need to. Residual heat from the hot pan will finish the job and give you perfect eggs every time!

Substitution tip
Part of what makes this recipe so flavorful is the use of fresh green herbs. If you have none on hand, substitute: ½ teaspoon dried parsley, ½ teaspoon dried chives, and ¼ teaspoon dried thyme leaves. The flavor will be similar but less pronounced.

Dairy-Free

Gluten-Free

Grain-Free

Nut-Free

Active time:

25 minutes

Total time:

30 minutes

Ingredient tip

So, what exactly is Canadian bacon? American bacon is made from smoked and cured pork belly, which is fatty (and delicious!), but nevertheless should be eaten in moderation. Canadian bacon is made from the other side of the pig (it's pork back that's been cured, smoked, and thickly sliced—and there's a lot less fat back there).

Maple-Mustard Canadian Bacon

☑ *Extra Quick* ★ *Serves 4*

Canadian bacon is leaner than its American cousin. A maple and Dijon glaze amps up the sweet and sharp flavors of this porky protein that's a lot more than "just ham." Along with the Bar-Raising Eggs Benedict (page 37), this bacon makes any breakfast more exciting.

8 Canadian bacon slices

¼ cup pure maple syrup

2 tablespoons Dijon mustard

1 Preheat the oven to 350°F. Line a sheet pan with aluminum foil.

2 Arrange the Canadian bacon slices on the prepared sheet pan.

3 In a small bowl, stir together the maple syrup and mustard. Generously coat both sides of each piece of bacon with the mixture.

4 Bake for 15 to 20 minutes, or until the bacon is crispy and glazed. Remove the bacon from the oven, cool slightly, and serve immediately.

Aloha Oatmeal Bites

Serves 6

Give your morning a tropical twist with these baked oatmeal bites! Pineapple, coconut, macadamia nuts, and banana pack this to-go breakfast with lots of fiber and flavor. Plus, they're flourless!

1 cup rolled oats

2 large eggs

2 ripe bananas, mashed

1 (8-ounce) can all-natural crushed pineapple, well drained

$\frac{3}{4}$ cup unsweetened shredded coconut

$\frac{1}{2}$ cup macadamia nuts, roughly chopped

$\frac{1}{4}$ cup honey, or agave nectar

2 tablespoons coconut oil

1 teaspoon vanilla extract

1 Preheat the oven to 350°F. Line a 12-well muffin tin with paper or silicone liners. Set aside.

2 In a medium bowl, combine the oats, eggs, bananas, pineapple, coconut, macadamia nuts, honey, coconut oil, and vanilla extract. Stir to mix the ingredients thoroughly.

3 Using a ¼-cup measuring cup, scoop the batter evenly into the prepared muffin wells. Press each scoop with the back of a spoon. You should be able to fit two scoops in each well.

4 Bake for 25 to 30 minutes, or until the batter is firm and the edges of the bites are a nice golden brown.

5 Remove the bites from the oven and let cool for at least 5 minutes before serving. The bites will come out of their liners more cleanly when they are completely cool.

🔖

Gluten-Free
Vegetarian

🕐

Active time:
10 minutes

Total time:
45 minutes

Preparation tip
To mash barely ripe bananas, microwave the banana halves for 1 minute. They will soften and sweeten up and mash more easily. Just make sure they aren't too hot when you mix them in. Or, to avoid this completely, use extra-extra-ripe bananas!

Vegetarian

Active time:
20 minutes

Total time:
1 hour

Cooking tip
To let food rest means to set it aside for a specified amount of time before cutting into it and serving. Meats, baked goods, and layered foods, like lasagna, are often rested to let juices reabsorb into the meats, layers solidify for easier serving, etc.

Apricot and Brie French Toast

Serves 8

Honey-poached apricots and creamy Brie make this baked French toast delectable. Because Brie is a rich cheese and is generally considered a bit fancy, save this dish for special occasions. Almond milk helps lighten the batter.

2 tablespoons unsalted butter

4 large eggs

2 cups unsweetened almond milk

5 tablespoons honey, divided

1 teaspoon vanilla extract

1 teaspoon ground cinnamon

Salt

1 cup water

1 cup dried apricots

1 loaf brioche, cut into ¾-inch-thick slices

6 ounces Brie cheese, thinly sliced

Sliced almonds, for garnish (optional)

1. Preheat the oven to 350°F. Coat a 9-by-13-inch baking dish with butter. Set aside.
2. In a large liquid measuring cup or bowl, whisk the eggs, almond milk, 2 tablespoons of honey, the vanilla extract, cinnamon, and a pinch of salt until well combined.
3. Meanwhile, in a medium saucepan over high heat, combine the remaining 3 tablespoons of honey and the water. Bring to a boil and reduce the heat to simmer. Add the apricots and simmer for at least 15 minutes, or until the apricots are plump.
4. In the prepared baking dish, layer the bread and cheese in slightly overlapping layers—don't worry if it's not perfect. Pour the egg mixture over the Brie and brioche slices. Let the custard absorb into the bread.

5 Pour the poached apricots and their honey syrup over everything. Lightly press everything down into the pan.

6 Bake uncovered for 25 minutes or until the bread is fluffy and golden brown and the Brie is melted. The syrup will be bubbling slightly at the edges.

7 Sprinkle the toast with the almonds (if using) and bake for 5 minutes more.

8 Remove from the oven and let it rest for 5 minutes before slicing and serving.

Active time:
35 minutes

Total time:
1 hour, 20 minutes

Preparation tip
If you can only find hazelnuts with their skins, you can remove them yourself. It's not hard; it just takes some time. To skin the hazelnuts, put them on a rimmed baking sheet and toast them in a 375°F oven for 8 to 10 minutes, or until fragrant. Remove them from the oven and let cool slightly so they can be handled. Place the nuts in a clean kitchen towel and rub them together in the towel to remove most of the skins. Alternatively, blanch the hazelnuts in boiling water with 1 tablespoon baking soda (the water will be black!) for about 3 minutes. Drain, cool slightly, and rub off the skins in the same manner.

Cranberry, Chocolate, and Hazelnut Granola

Makes about 4 cups

This granola is great to make in one batch and use throughout the week as cereal, in parfaits, or to top the Blueberry-Acai Bowl (page 20). Cranberries, dark chocolate, and hazelnuts conjure up the best trail mixes without ramping up the sugar and additives. Chia seeds add a boost of protein to this fiber- and antioxidant-packed treat.

½ cup coconut oil

¼ cup honey, or agave nectar

3 cups rolled oats

4 ounces hazelnuts, blanched (skinned), chopped (see tip)

4 ounces almonds, chopped

¼ cup chia seeds

Kosher salt

½ cup dried cranberries

3½ ounces dark chocolate, chopped

1 Preheat the oven to 325°F and position a rack in the middle of the oven. Line a sheet pan with parchment paper. Set aside.

2 In a glass measuring cup, combine the coconut oil and honey. Melt this mixture in the microwave at high power for 1 to 2 minutes, or until liquid. Stir to combine and set aside.

3 In a large bowl, combine the oats, hazelnuts, almonds, chia seeds, and a pinch of salt. Pour the coconut oil and honey mixture over the oat mixture and stir until all the oats and nuts are well coated. Pour the granola in a single layer on the prepared sheet pan.

4 Bake for 15 minutes. Stir the granola and re-flatten it into a single layer. Bake for 10 to 15 minutes more, or until lightly golden and fragrant.

5 Remove the granola from the oven (it will still feel pretty soft to the touch). Let cool almost completely, at least 30 minutes.

6   Sprinkle the granola with the cranberries and dark chocolate, pressing them lightly into the granola. Let cool completely.

7   Break the granola into pieces. If you prefer larger clusters, use your hands. If you prefer smaller clusters, use a spoon to break it up well. Store in an airtight container for up to a few weeks (though it likely won't last that long).

Active time:
25 minutes

Total time:
40 minutes

Ingredient tip
To make your own pumpkin pie spice, in a small lidded jar, combine 4 parts ground cinnamon, 2 parts ground nutmeg, and 1 part each ground cloves and ground ginger. (For example: 4 teaspoons ground cinnamon, 2 teaspoons ground nutmeg, 1 teaspoon ground cloves, and 1 teaspoon ground ginger.) You can always make more or less, maintaining this ratio. Use what's needed and store the rest in an airtight container at room temperature.

Pumpkin Pancakes
with Fig-Maple Syrup

Serves 6

These pancakes are perfect for chillier fall and winter mornings. Plus, the batter is made in the blender, so you can whip them up in minutes. Fig-maple syrup gives these pancakes a festive twist, and pumpkin seeds (also known as pepitas) add texture.

For the fig-maple syrup

½ **cup fig preserves**

⅓ **cup pure maple syrup**

¼ **cup cold water**

For the pancakes

1½ **cups rolled oats**

2 large eggs

½ **cup cold water**

⅓ **cup all-natural or organic canned pumpkin purée**

1½ **tablespoons pure maple syrup**

1 teaspoon baking powder

½ **teaspoon pumpkin pie spice (see tip)**

4 tablespoons butter or coconut oil

Toasted pepitas (pumpkin seeds), for topping

To make the fig-maple syrup

In a small saucepan over medium-low heat, combine the fig preserves, maple syrup, and water. Cook for 7 to 8 minutes, stirring occasionally to prevent burning, until warmed. Keep warm or set aside.

To make the pancakes

1 Preheat a griddle or medium skillet over medium to medium-low heat.

2 In a blender, combine the oats, eggs, water, and pumpkin. Blend for 1 minute, or until well mixed and the oats are partially blended. The remaining oats should be the size of medium crumbs.

3 Add the maple syrup, baking powder, and pumpkin pie spice. Blend for about 2 minutes, or until well mixed.

4 Add 1½ teaspoons of butter to the hot griddle to melt.

5 Using a ¼-cup measuring cup, add portions of batter to the hot pan. Do not crowd the pan with too many pancakes. Cook the pancakes on one side for 2 to 3 minutes, or until thick bubbles pop in the center. Using a spatula, carefully flip the pancakes and cook for 2 to 3 minutes more. Remove and keep warm. Repeat with the remaining butter and batter.

6 Serve a stack of 2 to 3 pancakes topped with warm fig-maple syrup and sprinkled with toasted pepitas.

Gluten-Free

Nut-Free

Vegetarian

Active time:
30 minutes

Total time:
40 minutes

Variation tip
Don't scramble the eggs. Instead add ½ cup salsa in step 7 (instead of the eggs) and fry the eggs separately. Top each serving with 1 fried egg and you've nearly got another Mexican staple, *chilaquiles*.

Migas de Madre

Serves 4

Migas is a Mexican dish comprising scrambled eggs, veggies, cheese, and flash-fried tortilla strips. To be clear, no one in my family is Mexican. But that didn't stop my mom from making this mainstay for weekend breakfasts (or even dinners). Migas will always be in my memories, and this recipe is adapted from my mother's.

2 tablespoons vegetable oil

10 small yellow or white corn tortillas, cut into long strips

1 onion, cut into medium dice

1 bell pepper, any color, cut into medium dice

1 large zucchini, cut into large dice

1½ teaspoons dried oregano

1 teaspoon garlic powder

½ teaspoon ground cumin

Kosher salt

Freshly ground black pepper

5 ounces (about ½ wheel) queso fresco, diced

4 large eggs

⅓ cup warm water

Organic salsa, for garnish (optional)

Chopped avocado, for garnish (optional)

1 Heat the vegetable oil in a wide-bottomed sauté pan or skillet over medium-high heat until it shimmers.

2 Add the tortilla strips and sauté for 3 to 4 minutes, or until light golden and crispy.

3 Turn the heat to medium-low. Add the onion to the tortillas and sauté for 2 minutes, or until translucent.

4 Add the bell pepper and zucchini and sauté for 2 minutes more.

5 Stir in the oregano, garlic powder, and cumin, and season with salt and pepper.

6 Sprinkle on the queso fresco and sauté for 2 minutes, stirring as you go.

7 In a small bowl, whisk the eggs and warm water until well beaten. Add the eggs to the pan. Cook the eggs for about 5 minutes, stirring occasionally, or until they reach your desired doneness.

8 Spoon some migas on a plate and top with salsa and chopped avocado (if using).

Active time:

25 minutes

Total time:

30 minutes

Variation tip

Add some eggs into the hash. After stirring in the cooked turkey (step 5), make two wells in the center of the hash with the back of a large spoon. Distribute the Gouda cheese around each well and crack 1 egg into each. Season the eggs with salt and pepper, cover the skillet, and cook on medium-low heat for at least 4 minutes until the egg whites are cooked and the yolks have begun to thicken. Serve the whole skillet at the table.

Gouda, Apple, and Sweet Potato Hash

☑ **Extra Quick** ★ *Serves 4*

Fantastic fall staples combine in this easy breakfast hash. Tart apple, tasty sweet potatoes, and ground turkey mix with smoky Gouda cheese, herbs, and spices for a wholesome, hearty dish.

1 tablespoon extra-virgin olive oil

8 ounces ground turkey

2 medium sweet potatoes, peeled and cut into medium dice

1 Granny Smith apple, peeled and cut into medium dice

1 tablespoon dried sage

½ teaspoon ground cinnamon

Kosher salt

Freshly ground black pepper

1 cup water

½ cup grated Gouda cheese

1 Heat the olive oil in a wide-bottomed skillet over medium-high heat, until it shimmers.

2 Add the ground turkey and cook for about 5 minutes, breaking it up with the back of a spoon, until cooked through and no longer pink. Transfer the cooked turkey to a bowl and set aside.

3 Return the skillet to the heat and add the sweet potatoes. Sauté for about 3 minutes, or until they begin to develop some color.

4 Add the apple, sage, and cinnamon, and season with salt and pepper. Stir to combine. Reduce the heat to medium-low. Add the water to the skillet and cook for 7 to 10 minutes, or until the potatoes and apples are fork-tender, stirring occasionally.

5 Stir in the cooked turkey. Sprinkle the Gouda cheese over the hash and stir lightly to mix.

Scallion and Soy Omelet
with Radishes

☑ **Extra Quick** ★ **Serves 1**

Asian-inspired flavors meld with classic French technique to make this quick omelet. Soy sauce gives the omelet an umami (savory) finish and thin, crisp slices of red radish wake up your palate.

1 red radish, root and top trimmed, very thinly sliced

3 large eggs

2 tablespoons warm water

2 scallions, green and some white parts, thinly sliced

1 tablespoon low-sodium soy sauce

2 tablespoons unsalted butter

Kosher salt

1. Fill a small bowl with cold water and add some ice cubes. Drop in the radish slices and let soak for 15 minutes. Drain and dry the radish.
2. In a small bowl, whisk the eggs and warm water until well beaten. Add the scallions and soy sauce and whisk to combine.
3. In a medium (8-inch) nonstick skillet over medium-low heat, melt the butter until it foams.
4. Add the egg mixture to the skillet. Cook for about 1 minute, stirring the eggs with a heatproof rubber spatula to form sheets of egg curd. When little liquid egg remains, tilt the pan in a circle to create a flat omelet. Cook for 1 minute more. Season with salt.
5. Fold one end of the omelet into the center of the pan, then fold that edge over on itself to create an omelet folded in thirds. Let sit in the skillet for 30 seconds. Turn the omelet out onto a plate and garnish with radish slices.

🔖 Nut-Free
Vegetarian

🕐 **Active time:**
10 minutes

Total time:
20 minutes

Cooking tip

As with making scrambled eggs, the key to a great omelet is control. If the eggs seem to be cooking too quickly, remove the pan from the heat for a few seconds. If you're not comfortable cooking the eggs quickly, proceed with a slightly lower temperature. Proper execution is more important than speed.

Active time:
35 minutes

Total time:
40 minutes

Ingredient tip
To clean leeks, remove and discard the dark green leaves and the root end. Halve the leeks lengthwise and thoroughly rinse between the layers until no sand or dirt is visible. Dry and prepare as instructed.

Mushrooms absorb liquid easily and quickly. Therefore, the best way to clean them is by wiping them off with a damp brush or paper towel to remove any dirt or grime.

Roasted Corn and Mushroom Frittata

Serves 6

Making a frittata is easy and a perfect option for brunch with or without company. This one combines sweet corn, mild leek, and earthy mushrooms with smoky and tangy cheese for a decadent dish.

2 cups yellow corn kernels, fresh or frozen

8 ounces cremini mushrooms, sliced, stems trimmed and discarded (see tip)

1 leek, halved lengthwise, washed well, and thinly sliced crosswise (light green and white parts, see tip)

3 tablespoons extra-virgin olive oil, divided

Kosher salt

Freshly ground black pepper

6 large eggs

¼ cup milk

1 tablespoon unsalted butter

¼ cup grated smoked provolone cheese

¼ cup goat cheese crumbles

1 teaspoon chopped fresh thyme leaves

1 Preheat the oven to 450°F and position a rack in the top third of the oven. Line a sheet pan with aluminum foil.

2 Spread the corn, mushrooms, and leek in a single layer on the prepared sheet pan. Drizzle with 2 tablespoons of olive oil and season with salt and pepper. Roast for 20 to 25 minutes, or until the vegetables have browned somewhat and cooked down. Remove from the oven and set aside on a heatproof surface to cool.

3 In a medium bowl, whisk the eggs and milk. Season the egg mixture with salt and pepper.

4 Place a large, wide-bottomed, ovenproof skillet over medium heat and add the remaining tablespoon of olive oil and the butter to melt.

5 Pour one-third of the eggs into the skillet. Cook, stirring, for about 20 seconds.

6 Add the cooked vegetables on top of the eggs and top the vegetables with the remaining egg mixture, making sure all the vegetables are surrounded by the egg. Cook for about 1 minute.

7 Sprinkle on the provolone cheese, goat cheese, and thyme, and season with pepper.

8 Reduce the heat to medium-low and cook for no more than 2 minutes. The frittata should be almost set, but the top will still be a little runny.

9 Transfer the skillet to the oven and bake for 4 to 5 minutes, or until the top is set and golden brown. Remove from the oven and let rest for about 2 minutes.

10 Release the frittata from the pan using a rubber spatula, sliding it under the edges of the frittata. Slide the whole frittata onto a cutting board, cut into 6 pieces (or more), and serve immediately. Alternatively, cut the frittata in the skillet and serve.

Gluten-Free

Grain-Free

Nut-Free

Vegetarian

Active time:

5 minutes

Total time:

15 minutes

Cooking tip

If you don't have a blender, make the hollandaise in a heat-proof bowl set over a pot of simmering water. Whisk the ingredients (step 1) until the eggs thicken, then add the water (it doesn't have to be hot) and melted butter. Fold in the yogurt, and you're done!

Healthier Hollandaise

☑ **Extra Quick** ★ **Makes about 2 cups**

Hollandaise is a staple for fancier breakfasts and brunches. Traditional hollandaise, however, contains lots of butter and can be rich. This peppery sauce lightens it up by substituting Greek yogurt for most of the butter, which is lower in fat and higher in protein.

4 large egg yolks, at room temperature

Juice of 1 lemon

2 teaspoons white wine vinegar

2 teaspoons peppercorns

1 teaspoon kosher salt

¼ cup nearly boiling water

4 tablespoons unsalted butter, melted

1 cup plain low-fat Greek yogurt, at room temperature

1 In a blender, combine the egg yolks, lemon juice, vinegar, and peppercorns. Blend to break up the peppercorns into a coarse grind. Add the salt and blend to combine.

2 With the blender running on low, slowly drizzle in 1 tablespoon of hot water. This will warm the eggs so the remaining hot water does not scramble them. Continue adding the hot water slowly in a thin, steady stream. When no water remains, blend for 1 minute more.

3 With the blender still running, slowly drizzle in the melted butter. Blend for 30 seconds to incorporate.

4 Add the yogurt and blend until the mixture is combined and homogenous. Stir well and use immediately.

Bar-Raising Eggs Benedict

Serves 4

Sweet and sharp Canadian bacon, savory roasted tomatoes, and peppery arugula elevate this brunch classic from standard to spectacular. Plus, the Healthier Hollandaise (page 36) makes this indulgent breakfast something to enjoy more often.

1 beefsteak tomato, thickly sliced

Extra-virgin olive oil

Kosher salt

Freshly ground black pepper

2 tablespoons white wine vinegar

4 large eggs

2 English muffins, halved and toasted

4 slices Maple-Mustard Canadian Bacon (page 22)

⅓ cup baby arugula

1 recipe Healthier Hollandaise (page 36), for serving

1 Preheat the oven to 350°F. Line a sheet pan with aluminum foil. Line a plate with a paper towel and set aside.

2 Place the tomato slices in a single layer on the prepared sheet pan. Drizzle them with olive oil and generously season both sides with salt and pepper. Roast for 25 to 30 minutes, or until slightly caramelized and a bit shrunken. Remove the pan from the oven and set aside on a heatproof surface.

3 Meanwhile, bring a medium pot about three-quarters full of water to a boil over high heat. Reduce the heat so the water is just below a simmer. Add the vinegar and stir.

Continued ▸

🔖

Nut-Free

🕐

Active time:
35 minutes

Total time:
45 minutes

Cooking tip
If you make the Canadian bacon at the same time as the tomato and poached eggs, cook the Canadian bacon on the same tray, at the same time, with the roasted tomatoes.

Bar-Raising Eggs Benedict Continued

4 Crack an egg into a small ramekin or dish. Stir the water again in a circular motion to create a whirlpool. Quickly dip the ramekin and pour the egg into the center of the whirlpool. Let the egg white wrap around the yolk. Poach for 2 to 3 minutes. Using a slotted spoon, transfer the egg to the prepared plate. Repeat with the remaining eggs, creating a new whirlpool each time.

5 On each of 4 serving plates, place a toasted English muffin half. Add 1 slice of roasted tomato, 1 slice of Canadian bacon, and top with arugula.

6 Perch the poached egg on top of the arugula and spoon the hollandaise over the top. Season with pepper and serve immediately.

3

SALADS and SOUPS

Gluten-Free
Grain-Free
Vegetarian

Active time:
20 minutes

Total time:
35 minutes

Ingredient tip
Use a good-quality Parmesan cheese, either in a block or shaved, not the powdered, pre-grated stuff found on the pasta aisle. Or substitute feta crumbles to give this raw salad a Greek twist.

Zucchini Salad
with Pine Nuts

Serves 4

Fresh, crunchy zucchini provides the base for this colorful, easy salad. Toasted pine nuts and shaved Parmesan offer nutty and salty notes for an altogether delicious combination!

For the vinaigrette

2 tablespoons freshly squeezed grapefruit juice

Kosher salt

Freshly ground black pepper

¼ cup extra-virgin olive oil

For the salad

¼ cup pine nuts

2 zucchini, ends trimmed

2 yellow squash, ends trimmed

2 ounces Parmigiano-Reggiano cheese, shaved

To make the vinaigrette

Place the grapefruit juice in a small bowl or large glass measuring cup and season it with salt and pepper. Whisk to combine. While whisking, add the olive oil in a slow, steady stream, whisking until blended. Set aside.

To make the salad

1 Fill a medium bowl with ice and water. Set aside.

2 In a small dry skillet over medium-high heat, toast the pine nuts until lightly browned and fragrant, no more than 3 minutes. Transfer to a small bowl and set aside to cool.

3 With a vegetable peeler, working over the ice water, shave across the zucchini and yellow squash lengthwise, making long, wide, strips. Refrigerate the vegetables for 10 minutes to crisp.

4 Drain and completely dry the zucchini and squash. Dry the bowl and return the vegetables to it.

5 Add the vinaigrette and toss to coat.

6 Sprinkle on the pine nuts.

7 Top with the Parmesan shavings and lightly toss to combine.

Active time:
8 minutes

Total time:
30 minutes

Serving tip
Spoon this salad onto some lettuce leaves for a light but protein-packed snack, or make a chickpea salad sandwich with some toasted bread.

Smashed Chickpea and Celery Salad

☑ **Extra Quick** ☆ *Makes about 2 cups*

This salad features chickpeas two ways for complex texture with crunchy celery, grassy dill, sweet golden raisins, and a creamy dressing to bind it all together. It's a salad you can gobble up in the same time it takes to make—merely minutes.

For the dressing

2 tablespoons light mayonnaise

2 tablespoons plain, low-fat Greek yogurt

2 tablespoons white wine vinegar

1 tablespoon Dijon mustard

1½ teaspoons extra-virgin olive oil

¾ teaspoon kosher salt

¾ teaspoon freshly ground black pepper

⅓ cup chopped fresh dill

For the salad

¾ cup golden raisins

1 cup water

1 (15-ounce) can all-natural chickpeas, drained

4 celery stalks, cut into small dice

Kosher salt

Freshly ground black pepper

To make the dressing

In a small bowl, whisk the mayonnaise, yogurt, vinegar, mustard, olive oil, salt, and pepper until combined. Stir in the dill. Set aside.

To make the salad

1   In a small bowl, combine the raisins and water. Let soak for about 10 minutes, or until raisins are plumped.

2 Evenly divide the chickpeas between 1 small bowl and 1 medium bowl. Using a fork or potato masher, roughly mash the chickpeas in the medium bowl.

3 Add the celery to the mashed chickpeas and stir to combine.

4 Drain the raisins.

5 Fold in the whole chickpeas and plumped raisins.

6 Pour the dressing over the salad and mix well. Taste and season with salt and pepper, as needed. Serve either immediately or refrigerate for at least 20 minutes to chill.

Nut-Free

Active time:
20 minutes

Total time:
30 minutes

Variation tip
For a protein boost, add my Lemon, Rosemary, and Garlic Chicken Breasts (see page 72). For the dressing, you can add 1 teaspoon anchovy paste or 2 anchovy filets (minced) for more flavor, or 1 teaspoon horseradish for extra sharpness. If you prefer to substitute store-bought croutons, use 2 to 3 cups.

Shaved Brussels Sprout Caesar

☑ *Extra Quick* ⋆ *Serves 3 to 4*

This Caesar salad uses shaved Brussels sprouts to add texture to the standard romaine lettuce. Homemade croutons and dressing turn the ordinary into the extraordinary. Plus, because the dressing is yogurt-based, the fat and calories of a typical Caesar are greatly reduced. If you're pressed for time, use all-natural store-bought croutons.

For the Caesar dressing

½ cup plain, low-fat Greek yogurt

2 tablespoons extra-virgin olive oil

2 garlic cloves, minced

Juice of 1 lemon

1 tablespoon Worcestershire sauce

1½ teaspoons Dijon mustard

¼ cup freshly grated Parmesan cheese

Kosher salt

Freshly ground black pepper

For the salad

2 heads romaine lettuce, chopped

12 ounces Brussels sprouts, trimmed and shaved or thinly sliced

2 tablespoons extra-virgin olive oil

1 garlic clove, minced

½ baguette, ciabatta, semolina, or other crusty bread, cut into medium dice

Kosher salt

Freshly ground black pepper

¼ cup freshly grated Parmesan cheese, plus more for garnish (optional)

To make the Caesar dressing

In a small bowl, whisk the yogurt, olive oil, garlic, lemon juice, Worcestershire sauce, mustard, and Parmesan cheese until smooth and pourable. If the dressing is too thick, add water as needed to adjust the consistency. Taste and season with salt and pepper, as needed. Set aside.

To make the salad

1 Preheat the oven to 400°F and position a rack in the middle of the oven. Line a sheet pan with aluminum foil. Set aside.

2 In a large bowl, combine the romaine and Brussels sprouts.

3 In a small saucepan over medium heat, combine the olive oil and garlic. Heat for about 1 minute, or until fragrant. Set aside.

4 Spread the bread cubes on the prepared sheet pan. Pour the garlic olive oil over the bread and season it with salt and pepper. Toss the cubes to coat in the oil.

5 Bake for 8 to 10 minutes, or until golden brown and crispy. Remove the croutons from the oven and place them onto the salad.

6 Sprinkle over the Parmesan cheese. Add as much dressing as desired. Toss to coat.

7 Serve garnished with more Parmesan cheese, as desired, and any remaining dressing on the side.

Dairy-Free
Vegetarian

Active time:
15 minutes

Total time:
20 minutes

Variation tip
Top this salad with a protein, such as Garlic, Cilantro, and Lime Chicken Breasts (page 74) for a complete meal.

Asian Slaw
with Mandarin Oranges

☑ *Extra Quick ★ Serves 4*

This light, refreshing Asian slaw salad is packed with fresh veggies and lots of flavor. Mandarin oranges offer a burst of sweetness, whereas peanuts, soy, and sesame amp up the umami flavors. Fresh cilantro boosts the freshness.

½ head Napa cabbage, thinly sliced into ribbons

2 carrots, cut into thin matchsticks

1 red bell pepper, julienned

⅓ cup fresh cilantro leaves

½ cup roasted, salted peanuts, chopped

3 tablespoons low-sodium soy sauce

Juice of 2 limes

2 tablespoons toasted sesame oil

1 tablespoon honey

1 (15-ounce) can all-natural mandarin oranges (in water), drained

1 In a large bowl, combine the cabbage, carrots, red bell pepper, and cilantro. Lightly toss to combine the ingredients.

2 Add the peanuts, soy sauce, lime juice, sesame oil, and honey, and toss to combine and coat.

3 Gently fold in the mandarin oranges so as not to break them up too much. Serve immediately.

Mary's Vegetable Stew

Serves 6 to 8

This recipe comes from a close family friend, Mary Clarke, who always cooks it for us whenever we come to visit. This hearty vegetable stew is sure to fill you up any time of year, though it is particularly comforting in winter. Use the best vegetables you can find for the best stew, and make enough for leftovers.

2 large onions, cut into medium dice

4 large carrots, cut into medium dice

4 celery stalks, cut into medium dice

2 red bell peppers, cut into medium dice

12 ounces green beans, trimmed and halved

8 ounces white mushrooms, stemmed, and halved

1 (28-ounce) can organic diced tomatoes with their juice

2 zucchini, cut into medium dice

1 (24-ounce) jar organic marinara sauce

2 rosemary sprigs

Kosher salt

Freshly ground black pepper

1 In a large stockpot over medium heat, add the onions, carrots, and celery. Cook for 3 to 4 minutes, or until the onions start to become translucent.

2 Add the red bell peppers, green beans, mushrooms, and tomatoes. Cook for 4 minutes.

3 Stir in the zucchini, marinara sauce, and rosemary. Bring the stew to a boil and reduce the heat to medium-low. Cook for about 25 minutes, or until the vegetables are fork-tender, stirring occasionally to prevent burning.

4 Remove and discard the rosemary. Stir one last time. Taste and season with salt and pepper, as needed.

Gluten-Free
Grain-Free
Nut-Free
Vegan

Active time:
35 minutes

Total time:
55 minutes

Serving tip
This stew is perfect with a nice, crusty bread and a few slices of fresh mozzarella or a little bit of grated Parmesan cheese.

Nut-Free
Vegetarian

Active time:
35 minutes

Total time:
45 minutes

Ingredient tip
Farro is a whole grain derived from wheat. If you can't find it, dried barley or quinoa makes a fine substitute, though not quite as nutty tasting. And you can always use regular balsamic instead of white balsamic, but the salad will have a slightly darker look.

Peach and Mozzarella Farro Salad

Serves 5 to 6

This salad is perfect for summertime, featuring sweet, succulent peaches, fresh corn, bright red onion, balsamic vinegar, peppery basil, and creamy mozzarella. Plus, it can be made in advance and served later.

For the dressing

2 ⅓ tablespoons white balsamic vinegar

1 ⅓ teaspoons honey

Kosher salt

Freshly ground black pepper

¼ cup extra-virgin olive oil

⅓ cup thinly sliced (chiffonade) fresh basil

For the salad

1 cup whole-grain farro

2 ¼ cups water

1 teaspoon kosher salt, plus more as needed

⅓ red onion, finely diced

1 (29-ounce) can peaches in their own juice, drained and rinsed well, cut into medium dice

1 cup yellow corn kernels, fresh or frozen and thawed

8 ounces fresh mozzarella pearls

Freshly ground black pepper

To make the dressing

1 In a small bowl, combine the vinegar and honey and season with salt and pepper. Whisk to blend.

2 While whisking, slowly add the olive oil in a thin, steady stream, whisking until blended.

3 Add the basil and toss to coat. Set aside.

To make the salad

1 In a medium saucepan over medium-high heat, combine the farro, water, and salt, and bring to a boil. Once boiling, reduce the heat to medium-low, cover the pan, and simmer the farro until tender, at least 30 minutes.

2 Meanwhile, soak the red onion in a bowl of ice water for at least 15 minutes (this will make it less strong and bitter).

3 Drain the farro in a colander. Rinse with cool water, drain again, and transfer to a serving bowl.

4 Drain the red onion and add it to the farro, along with the peaches, corn, mozzarella cheese, and dressing. Toss to mix well. Taste and season with salt and pepper, as needed. Serve at room temperature.

Gluten-Free

Grain-Free

Vegetarian

Active time:

15 minutes

Total time:

25 minutes

Ingredient tip

If you can't find Cotija cheese, substitute feta cheese or ricotta salata, or any hard, salty, crumbly white cheese.

Warm Avocado Salad
with Pomegranate and Walnuts

☑ *Extra Quick* ⋆ *Serves 4*

When avocados are seared, they take on a sweet-and-smoky dimension in addition to their creaminess. Crunchy walnuts, sharp cheese, and tart bursts of pomegranate and lime complement the star ingredient. Loosely inspired by the traditional Mexican dish, *chiles en nogada*, which features pomegranate and a creamy walnut sauce, this indulgent treat both tastes great and is great for you.

For the chili-lime vinaigrette

Juice of 2 limes (about ⅓ cup)

2 tablespoons agave nectar

1 teaspoon chili powder

½ teaspoon ground cumin

Kosher salt

Freshly ground black pepper

¼ cup canola oil or grapeseed oil

For the salad

1 cup walnut halves

2 avocados, halved and pitted (see tip, page 19)

Kosher salt

Freshly ground black pepper

1 tablespoon canola oil, or grapeseed oil

8 ounces spring mix lettuce

5 ounces Cotija cheese, in large crumbles

4 ounces pomegranate seeds

To make the chili-lime vinaigrette

1 In a small bowl, combine the lime juice, agave, chili powder, and cumin, and season with salt and pepper. Whisk to blend.

2 While whisking, drizzle in the canola oil, whisking until blended. Taste and season with salt and pepper, as needed. Set aside.

To make the salad

1 In a dry skillet over medium heat, toast the walnuts until fragrant, no longer than 4 minutes. Transfer the walnuts to a plate and set aside to cool.

2 Using a spoon, scoop the avocado flesh from their skins. Halve each avocado half, cutting around the fruit. You should end up with two thick, round slices per scooped half. Season the avocado "steaks" generously with salt and pepper.

3 Return the skillet to medium-high heat and heat the canola oil until it shimmers.

4 Place the avocado slices, seasoned-side down, in the skillet. Sear for no more than 4 minutes, or until they have a golden brown crust. Flip and press the avocado slightly against the pan to sear the other side for 4 minutes. Transfer to a plate to cool briefly.

5 In a medium bowl, combine the cooled walnuts, spring mix, Cotija cheese, pomegranate seeds, and most of the chili-lime vinaigrette. Gently toss to combine.

6 Drizzle the seared avocado with the remaining vinaigrette.

7 Divide the salad among 4 plates and top each with 2 avocado "steaks." Serve immediately.

Active time:

25 minutes

Total time:

55 minutes

Ingredient tip

Butternut squash is a big vegetable and can be a bit difficult to handle. To make it more manageable, first halve it lengthwise with a chef's knife and remove the seeds using a spoon. Cut each half in half cross-wise and, working with one-fourth of the squash, slowly remove the thick skin using a vegetable peeler. Cut each peeled quarter as desired.

Basic Butternut Bisque

Serves 4

This squash soup recipe introduces the basic techniques behind any puréed soup. Master the basics, and you can transform any produce into something velvety smooth and satisfying. Feel free to switch up toppings, ingredients, and vegetables to suit the season or your tastes.

2 tablespoons extra-virgin olive oil

2 tablespoons unsalted butter

1 medium butternut squash, peeled and cut into medium dice

½ onion, peeled and cut into medium dice

6 cups low-sodium vegetable broth

Kosher salt

Freshly ground black pepper

⅓ cup heavy (whipping) cream

1 tablespoon pure maple syrup, plus more as needed

¼ teaspoon ground ginger

1 Heat the olive oil and butter in a large soup pot over medium heat, until melted. Stir to combine.

2 Add the butternut squash and onion. Stir to coat the vegetables with the oil and butter. Cover the pot and cook for 5 to 6 minutes, or until the vegetables start to soften, stirring occasionally.

3 Stir in the vegetable broth and generously season the soup with salt and pepper. Bring the soup to a boil, then reduce the heat to medium-low. Cook for about 20 minutes, or until the butternut squash is very fork-tender.

4   Using an immersion blender in the pot, purée the soup until it is velvety smooth. Alternatively, working in batches as needed, transfer the soup to a standard blender, only filling it about half-way, and blend until smooth. Pour all the soup back into the pot once it has been puréed. Turn the heat to low.

5   Stir in the cream, maple syrup, and ginger. Taste and season with salt and pepper, as needed. Cook for about 1 minute more, just to bring everything together.

Active time:
25 minutes

Total time:
40 minutes

Variation tip
Once you are a pro with this recipe, substitute any cool, refreshing fruits, vegetables, and herbs. Tomatillos, many sorts of melon, and strawberries are all ingredients to add to this gazpacho for a twist. Or keep it classic, but amp up the heat with some jalapeño.

Cooking tip
If you prefer, skip the roasting (steps 1 to 3). The flavor will be brighter and taste less of those roasted caramel notes.

Golden Gazpacho

Serves 4

This cool, fresh soup is golden two times over: once in its brilliant yellow color, and again in the golden edges that develop on the roasted tomatoes and peppers when roasted. Originally from the Andalusia region in Spain, gazpacho is the epitome of many chilled soups. A bowl of this soup would be perfect on a blazing summer afternoon.

- 20 ounces yellow cherry tomatoes, halved and divided, or 2 large yellow tomatoes, halved, seeded, and thickly sliced
- 2 yellow bell peppers, seeded and thickly sliced
- 2 teaspoons kosher salt, plus more as needed
- 1 teaspoon freshly ground black pepper, plus more as needed
- 6 tablespoons extra-virgin olive oil, divided
- 1 cucumber, peeled and cut into small dice, divided
- $\frac{1}{2}$ red onion, cut into medium dice, divided
- 1 slice stale crusty bread, roughly chopped
- 2 garlic cloves, smashed
- 2 tablespoons white wine vinegar, plus more as needed
- 2 tablespoons thinly sliced (chiffonade) fresh basil, plus more for garnish

1. Preheat the oven to 400°F and position a rack in the center of the oven. Line a sheet pan with aluminum foil.
2. Spread the cherry tomatoes and yellow bell peppers in an even layer on the prepared sheet pan. Generously season with salt and pepper and drizzle with 2 tablespoons of olive oil. Toss to coat.
3. Roast for 15 to 20 minutes, or until lightly golden and caramelized. Remove the pan from the oven and let the vegetables cool briefly.
4. Set aside ½ cup cucumber and ¼ cup red onion in a small bowl.
5. In a blender, combine the cooled tomatoes and bell peppers and the remaining cucumber. Purée until smooth.

6   Add the remaining red onion, bread, garlic, salt, and pepper to the blender. Purée for about 1 minute. Remove the blender cap from the lid. With the blender running, slowly drizzle in the remaining 4 tablespoons of olive oil. Thin the soup with water, as needed.

7   Add the vinegar and basil. Blend for 30 seconds to combine. Taste and season with more salt, pepper, or vinegar, as needed, until the soup is slightly zesty.

8   Let cool to room temperature, or refrigerate for at least 10 minutes before serving.

9   Garnish with more basil and a spoonful of the reserved cucumber and red onion.

Dairy-Free
Gluten-Free
Grain-Free
Nut-Free

Active time:
20 minutes

Total time:
45 minutes

Ingredient tip
You can find Thai green curry paste with the sauces in the Asian section of most grocery stores, or at specialty grocery markets.

Thai Edamame Soup
with Shrimp

Serves 4

This bright, zingy, creamy soup incorporates the flavors of Thailand, a boost of added protein from the edamame and shrimp, and a stunning green color. Plus, it's dairy-free and relatively quick to make.

1 to 2 tablespoons all-natural Thai green curry paste	*1 (13.5-ounce) can coconut milk, divided*
Zest of 1 lime	*1 tablespoon coconut oil*
Juice of 1 lime	*8 ounces peeled and deveined jumbo shrimp*
2 cups water	
2¼ cups frozen shelled edamame, divided	*Kosher salt*
	¼ cup fresh cilantro leaves, chopped

1 In a medium pot over medium heat, combine the curry paste, lime zest, and lime juice. Sauté for about 2 minutes, or until fragrant.

2 Stir in the water. Remove ½ cup of the liquid and set aside.

3 Add 2 cups of edamame to the pot. Cook for about 10 minutes, or until tender.

4 Stir in ½ cup of coconut milk.

5 Using an immersion blender in the pot, purée the soup until smooth. Alternatively, working in batches as needed, transfer the soup to a standard blender, filling about halfway full, purée until smooth and return the soup to the pot.

6 Stir in the remaining coconut milk and keep the soup warm over medium-low heat while you prepare the shrimp.

7 In a wide sauté pan or skillet over medium heat, combine the coconut oil and the shrimp. Sauté for about 2 minutes until the shrimp are just starting to blush pink on both sides.

8 Add the reserved broth, cover the pan, and turn the heat to medium-low. Steam the shrimp for 4 minutes, or until rosy and just slightly curled. Turn off the heat and set the pan aside—the residual heat from the pan will finish cooking the shrimp perfectly.

9 In a small microwaveable bowl, microwave the remaining ½ cup of edamame for 1 to 2 minutes on high power, or until thawed and warmed through.

10 Taste the soup and season with salt, as needed. Ladle the soup into bowls. Sprinkle with cilantro and edamame and carefully nestle 2 or 3 shrimp on top.

Dairy-Free
Nut-Free

Active time:
30 minutes

Total time:
55 minutes

Cooking tip
Deglazing is done by pouring a liquid into a hot pan and scraping the bottom of the pan to loosen and incorporate any browned bits.

Garlic-Herb Chicken Orzo Soup

Serves 4 to 5

Myriad herbs and the flavors of grapes and garlic make this soup taste of the French countryside. Perfect year-round or, of course, when recovering from an illness.

4 tablespoons extra-virgin olive oil, divided

2 tablespoons butter, divided

2 boneless, skinless chicken breasts

Kosher salt

Freshly ground black pepper

7 cups low-sodium chicken broth, divided

1 red bell pepper, julienned

1 onion, thinly sliced

2 garlic cloves, minced

1¼ teaspoons herbes de Provence

6 tablespoons white grape juice

2 tablespoons freshly squeezed lemon juice, or white wine vinegar

8 ounces orzo

Fresh parsley, for garnish

1 Heat 2 tablespoons of olive oil and 1 tablespoon of butter in a large sauté pan or skillet over medium-high heat, until the butter melts.

2 Season the chicken on both sides with salt and pepper and add it to the pan. Cook for 2 minutes per side.

3 Add 1 cup of chicken broth, lower the heat slightly, and cover the pan. Cook for 7 minutes, or until the chicken reaches an internal temperature of 165°F measured on an instant-read thermometer. Transfer the chicken to a plate and let sit for 2 minutes. Using two forks, shred the chicken.

4 In a large pot or Dutch oven over medium heat, heat the remaining 2 tablespoons of olive oil and 1 tablespoon of butter until the butter melts.

5 Add the red bell pepper, onion, garlic, herbes de Provence, 1 tea-spoon of salt, and ½ teaspoon of pepper. Sauté for about 5 min-utes, or until the onion is translucent, the garlic is fragrant, and the red pepper has begun to soften.

6 Pour in the grape juice and lemon juice to deglaze the pan (see tip), stirring with a wooden spoon to loosen any browned bits stuck to the bottom.

7 Add the shredded chicken and the remaining 6 cups of chicken broth. Bring the soup to a boil.

8 Add the orzo and lower the heat to simmer. Cook for about 10 minutes, or until the orzo is *al dente* (slightly chewy).

9 Taste and season with salt and pepper, as needed. Ladle the soup into bowls and garnish with parsley.

Active time:
35 minutes

Total time:
1 hour

Ingredient tip
If you have leftover chicken, especially leftover Garlic, Cilantro, and Lime Chicken Breasts (page 74), shred that and add it to the soup instead of prepping a fresh chicken breast.

Mexican Street Corn and Chicken Chowder

Serves 4 to 5

This chowder is inspired by the flavors of beloved Mexican *elote*, or street corn, which is grilled corn slathered in crema, cheese, and spices. This soup is creamy, smoky, and tangy all at once, and the grilled chicken adds another layer of texture.

4 tablespoons extra-virgin olive oil, divided

1 boneless, skinless chicken breast

Kosher salt

Freshly ground black pepper

2½ cups low-sodium chicken broth, divided

½ yellow onion, diced into small pieces

¾ teaspoon chili powder

¼ teaspoon cayenne pepper

2 cups yellow corn kernels, fresh or frozen

Juice of 1 lime

½ cup reduced-fat sour cream

Crumbled Cotija cheese, or feta cheese, for garnish (optional)

Fresh cilantro, for garnish (optional)

1 lime, cut into wedges

1 Heat 2 tablespoons of olive oil in a medium sauté pan or skillet over medium-high heat, until it shimmers.

2 Season the chicken on both sides with salt and pepper and add it to the pan. Cook for 2 minutes per side.

3 Add ½ cup of chicken broth, lower the heat slightly, and cover the pan. Cook for 7 minutes, or until the chicken reaches an internal temperature of 165°F measured on an instant-read thermometer. Transfer the chicken to plate and let sit for 2 minutes. Using two forks, shred the chicken.

4   Heat the remaining 2 tablespoons of olive oil in a large stockpot or Dutch oven over medium heat.

5   Add the onion, chili powder, and cayenne pepper. Stir to combine. Sauté for about 3 minutes, or until the onion is lightly browned.

6   Add the corn and sauté for 2 minutes.

7   Add the lime juice to deglaze the pan, stirring with a wooden spoon to loosen any browned bits stuck to the bottom. Taste and season with salt and pepper, as needed.

8   Add the remaining 2 cups of chicken broth. Bring the soup to a boil and reduce the heat to simmer. Cook for 15 minutes. Remove the pot from the heat.

9   Transfer a ladleful of the corn and chicken broth to a medium bowl. Stir in the sour cream until combined. Pour the sour cream mixture into the pot and stir until it's combined.

10 Stir in the shredded chicken. Ladle the soup into bowls and top with the Cotija and cilantro (if using). Serve with a lime wedge.

Active time:

35 minutes

Total time:

55 minutes

Variation tip

Other spring ingredients you could include in this soup are fava beans, watercress (for a sharper bite), and baby artichokes. If you want a smoky, meaty note in your soup, add 4 ounces diced, crisped pancetta (an Italian cured bacon) or regular bacon.

Minestrone Verde

Serves 4 to 5

A pot of primavera, this soup spotlights green spring ingredients and fresh grassy flavors. Creamy white beans offer body and Parmesan cheese provides some saltiness and depth.

---

2 tablespoons extra-virgin olive oil

4 parsnips, peeled and cut into medium dice

1 garlic clove, minced

Kosher salt

Freshly ground black pepper

1 bunch asparagus, ends trimmed and stalks cut into 1-inch pieces

8 cups low-sodium vegetable broth

1 (10-ounce) box frozen spinach, thawed and drained

1 Parmesan cheese rind

1 (15-ounce) can cannellini beans, drained and rinsed

Grated Parmesan cheese, for serving

---

1 Heat the olive oil in a large pot or Dutch oven over medium-low heat, until it shimmers.

2 Add the parsnips and garlic, and sauté for about 5 minutes, or until the parsnips start to soften. Season with salt and pepper.

3 Add the asparagus, and sauté for an additional 2 minutes.

4 Add the vegetable broth, and bring the soup to a boil.

5 Add the spinach and Parmesan rind. Reduce the heat to medium-low. Cook for 15 to 20 minutes, or until the parsnips and asparagus are fork-tender.

6 Pour half the white beans into a bowl. Add 2 tablespoons of broth from the pot and mash the beans with a fork until smooth. Stir the bean paste into the soup. Add the remaining white beans. Cook for 5 to 6 minutes.

7 Remove any remaining Parmesan cheese rind. Ladle the soup into bowls. Garnish with additional Parmesan cheese.

Lamb and Lentil Stew

Serves 4 to 5

Take a culinary trip to North Africa with this warm, comforting stew. Onion, cauliflower, ground lamb, and lentils simmer until super tender, and a toasted spice blend amps up the flavor. This stew is perfect for cold and chilly nights.

2 tablespoons canola oil, or grapeseed oil

1 tablespoon ground coriander

2 teaspoons ground cumin

¾ teaspoon caraway seeds

¾ teaspoon red pepper flakes

1 pound ground lamb

1 head cauliflower, stem trimmed, head cut into small florets

1 onion, cut into medium dice

2 garlic cloves, minced

Kosher salt

2 tablespoons all-natural tomato paste

4 cups low-sodium chicken broth, divided

1 cup split yellow or red lentils, rinsed, drained, and picked through for stones and debris

1. Heat the canola oil in a large heavy-bottomed stockpot or Dutch oven over medium-high heat, until it shimmers.
2. Sprinkle the coriander, cumin, caraway seeds, and red pepper flakes over the oil and toast for about 2 minutes, or until fragrant.
3. Add the ground lamb. Cook for about 8 minutes, stirring and breaking it up with the back of a spoon, until cooked through and no longer pink. Using a slotted spoon, transfer the cooked lamb to a plate and set aside.

Continued ▶

Dairy-Free
Nut-Free

Active time:
30 minutes

Total time:
1 hour

Variation tip
Not a fan of lamb? Substitute an equal amount of ground beef.

Serving tip
Serve with couscous and a dollop of yogurt to take things up a notch.

Lamb and Lentil Stew Continued

4 Return the pot to the stovetop and turn the heat to medium-low. Add the cauliflower, onion, garlic, and a generous pinch of salt. Sauté for 5 to 6 minutes, or until the onion is translucent and the cauliflower has begun to soften.

5 Stir in the tomato paste and cook for 2 minutes.

6 Add 2 cups of chicken broth to deglaze the pan, stirring with a wooden spoon to loosen any browned bits stuck to the bottom.

7 Stir the ground lamb back into the pot. Simmer for 5 minutes.

8 Stir in the remaining 2 cups of chicken broth and the lentils. Cook, uncovered, for 15 minutes, or until the cauliflower is fork-tender and the lentils are soft. Taste and season with salt, as needed. Serve immediately.

4 MAINS for ONE

Gluten-Free

Grain-Free

Nut-Free

Active time:

25 minutes

Total time:

1 hour

◇

Ingredient tip

Normally, cooking with three varieties of pepper in one recipe is unnecessary. Here, the black pepper is standard, the white pepper adds more heat, and paprika adds a nice smokiness. You can find all three on the spice aisle in many grocery stores. If you cannot find white pepper, omit it from the recipe.

Salt and Three Pepper Chicken Breasts

Serves 2

The boneless, skinless chicken breast is a staple of the modern American kitchen, as well as one of the healthiest and most versatile proteins. It's the protein I cook most often. Here's my mainstay recipe for when you need a chicken breast as a main dish or for another dish. Don't be fooled by its simplicity; this recipe is far from bland! Plus, a dip in a yogurt marinade tenderizes the chicken and keeps it moist while cooking.

$\frac{2}{3}$ **cup plain, low-fat Greek yogurt**

Juice of 1 lemon

1 teaspoon ground paprika

1$\frac{1}{2}$ teaspoons freshly ground black pepper

$\frac{1}{3}$ **teaspoon ground white pepper**

1 tablespoon kosher salt

2 boneless, skinless chicken breasts

1 In a medium bowl, stir together the yogurt, lemon juice, paprika, black and white peppers, and salt until combined.

2 Completely submerge the chicken in the marinade. Cover the bowl tightly with plastic wrap and refrigerate for at least 30 minutes, or up to 24 hours for extra tenderization.

3 Preheat the oven to 400°F. Line a sheet pan with aluminum foil and set aside.

4 Bring the chicken to room temperature. Remove the breasts from the marinade and place on the prepared sheet pan. Discard the excess marinade.

5   Bake for 15 to 18 minutes, or until the chicken is browned at the edges and the juices run *almost* clear when the chicken is pierced.

6   Remove the pan from the oven and tent the chicken with foil. Let rest for 5 to 7 minutes to let the juices redistribute, or until the chicken reaches an internal temperature of 165°F measured at the thickest part with an instant-read thermometer. The juices will now run clear.

7   Serve immediately, or cool to room temperature and refrigerate.

Dairy-Free
Gluten-Free
Grain-Free
Nut-Free

Active time:
25 minutes

Total time:
1 hour

Cooking tip
The marinade should not look oily when combined properly. It is more likely to combine correctly if you go slowly. When an oil and acid combine, they become emulsified. Massaging the marinade into the chicken helps ensure that the marinade permeates the meat.

Lemon, Rosemary, and Garlic Chicken Breasts

Serves 2

Classic flavors of lemon, rosemary, and garlic liven up this weeknight protein. The marinade comes together in minutes and pairs well with French and Italian food. Use the chicken as a stand-alone dish, or in salads, pastas, or soups.

Grated zest of 1 lemon

Juice of 1 lemon

2 garlic cloves, minced

2 tablespoons fresh rosemary leaves, chopped

1 teaspoon kosher salt, plus more as needed

$\frac{1}{2}$ teaspoon freshly ground black pepper, plus more as needed

$\frac{1}{4}$ cup extra-virgin olive oil

2 boneless, skinless chicken breasts

1   In a medium bowl, whisk the lemon zest, lemon juice, garlic, rosemary, salt, and pepper until combined.

2   While whisking, add the olive oil in a thin, steady stream, whisking until well blended and thick.

3   Place the chicken in a gallon-size resealable plastic bag and pour in the marinade. Seal the bag and massage the ingredients to combine. Refrigerate for at least 30 minutes or up to 24 hours.

4   Preheat the oven to 400°F. Line a sheet pan with aluminum foil and set aside.

5   Bring the chicken to room temperature. Remove the breasts from the marinade and place on the prepared sheet pan. Discard the excess marinade.

6   Bake for 15 to 18 minutes, or until the chicken is browned at the edges and the juices run *almost* clear.

7   Remove the pan from the oven and tent the chicken with foil. Let rest for 5 to 7 minutes to let the juices redistribute, or until the chicken reaches an internal temperature of 165°F measured at the thickest part with an instant-read thermometer. The juices will now run clear.

8   Serve immediately, or cool to room temperature and refrigerate.

Dairy-Free

Gluten-Free

Grain-Free

Nut-Free

Active time:

25 minutes

Total time:

1 hour

Variation tip

Add 1 teaspoon toasted sesame oil and substitute soy sauce for salt to make this an Asian-style marinade (which will no longer be Gluten-Free or Grain-Free); consider adding some red pepper flakes for a kick.

Garlic, Cilantro, and Lime Chicken Breasts

Serves 2

Garlic, cilantro, and lime is a versatile and slightly tropical flavor profile that pairs well with Asian and Latin cuisines.

Zest of 1½ limes

Juice of 1½ limes

¼ cup fresh cilantro, chopped

2 garlic cloves, minced

1 teaspoon kosher salt, plus more as needed

¼ teaspoon freshly ground black pepper, plus more as needed

¼ cup extra-virgin olive oil, or grapeseed oil

2 boneless, skinless chicken breasts

1 In a medium bowl, whisk the lime zest, lime juice, cilantro, garlic, salt, and pepper until combined.

2 While whisking, add the olive oil in a thin, steady stream, whisking until blended.

3 Place the chicken in a gallon-size resealable plastic bag and pour in the marinade. Seal the bag and massage the ingredients to combine. Refrigerate for at least 30 minutes or up to 24 hours.

4 Preheat the oven to 400°F. Line a sheet pan with aluminum foil and set aside.

5 Bring the chicken to room temperature. Remove the breasts from the marinade and place on the prepared sheet pan. Discard the excess marinade.

6 Bake for 15 to 18 minutes, or until the chicken is browned at the edges and the juices run *almost* clear.

7   Remove the pan from the oven and tent the chicken with foil. Let rest for 5 to 7 minutes to let the juices redistribute, or until the chicken reaches an internal temperature of 165°F measured at the thickest part with an instant-read thermometer. The juices will now run clear.

8   Serve immediately, or cool to room temperature and refrigerate.

Active time:
15 minutes

Total time:
20 minutes

Variation tip
Use whatever nuts or fruit you like. Apricots and pistachios would lend a Mediterranean twist, and cranberries and almonds are a bit more autumnal, but grapes and pecans are classic.

Toasted Chicken Salad Wrap

☑ **Extra Quick** ★ **Serves 1**

Fast, homemade, warm, and creamy chicken salad in a crisp tortilla with sweet grapes and crunchy pecans. What else could be as simple or satisfying?

½ shredded cooked chicken breast, such as Salt and Three Pepper Chicken Breasts (page 70)

¼ to ½ cup red or green seedless grapes, stemmed and halved

2 tablespoons plain, low-fat Greek yogurt

Juice of ¼ lemon

1½ teaspoons light mayonnaise

2 tablespoons finely chopped pecans

½ teaspoon poppy seeds

Kosher salt

Freshly ground black pepper

1 large whole-wheat tortilla

1 tablespoon extra-virgin olive oil

1   In a medium bowl, stir together the chicken, grapes, yogurt, lemon juice, mayonnaise, pecans, and poppy seeds. Taste and season with salt and pepper, as needed. Stir well to combine.

2   Heat the olive oil in a small skillet over medium heat, until it shimmers.

3   Spoon the chicken salad into the center of the lower third of the tortilla. Fold the end of the tortilla over the chicken salad. Fold in the sides and roll the tortilla into a cylinder.

4   Place the wrap in the skillet fold-side down, and panfry both sides for 1 to 2 minutes, or until golden brown and crispy. Transfer to a plate, halve, and serve.

Buffalo Chicken Grilled Cheese

☑️ *Extra Quick ☆ Serves 1*

Broiling this relatively rich sandwich, along with a few key substitutions and additions, lightens up what many consider the always delicious, but often unhealthy, classic: grilled cheese. Fresh carrot and celery amplify the crispiness, offering a bite of freshness.

2 ounces reduced-fat cream cheese, at room temperature, divided

2 slices multigrain bread

½ shredded cooked chicken breast such as Salt and Three Pepper Chicken Breasts (page 70)

2 tablespoons blue cheese, crumbled

1 teaspoon favorite hot sauce or more, to taste

1 celery stalk, thinly sliced with a vegetable peeler

1 carrot, thinly sliced with a vegetable peeler

1 Preheat the broiler.
2 Spread a small layer of cream cheese on both slices of bread.
3 In a small bowl, stir together the chicken, blue cheese, hot sauce, and remaining cream cheese.
4 On one bread slice, place the celery and carrot on the cream cheese.
5 Spoon the chicken mixture on top. Top with the other piece of bread, cream cheese-side down. Place the sandwich on a sheet pan.
6 Broil for 1 to 2 minutes, or until the bread is toasted. Flip the sandwich and broil the other side for 1 to 2 minutes more.
7 Turn off the oven, with the sheet tray and sandwich still inside, and cook for an additional 3 minutes to warm sandwich thoroughly.

🔖 Nut-Free

🕐 **Active time:**
15 minutes

Total time:
20 minutes

Cooking tip
Slicing the carrot and celery with a vegetable peeler is easy and can be accomplished by gliding the blade lengthwise along the vegetables. For extra crunch, crisp the carrot and celery in some ice water for about 10 minutes. Drain and dry before adding to the sandwich.

Gluten-Free

Grain-Free

Nut-Free

Active time:

15 minutes

Total time:

1 hour, 30 minutes

Ingredient tip

Garam masala is a classic Indian spice blend. It contains, among many other spices, black and white peppers, curry leaf, cinnamon, cumin, and cardamom.

Chicken and Cauliflower Skewers

Serves 2

Inspired by tikka, a South Asian style of cooking, this dish packs lots of smoky, sweet, and spicy flavor. A simple mint and cucumber raita cools things off. Be sure to soak your bamboo or wooden skewers in water for at least 1 hour before starting, or use metal skewers.

For the mint-cucumber raita

1 cucumber, grated and squeezed of excess moisture

½ cup plain, low-fat Greek yogurt

¼ cup fresh mint, thinly sliced

Kosher salt

Freshly ground black pepper

For the chicken and cauliflower skewers

1 cup plain, low-fat Greek yogurt

Juice of 1 lime

1½ tablespoons garam masala

1 tablespoon paprika

1 tablespoon kosher salt

Freshly ground black pepper

1 boneless, skinless chicken breast, cut into large chunks

½ head cauliflower, root removed, head cut into large florets

To make the mint-cucumber raita

In a small bowl, stir together the cucumber, yogurt, mint, salt, and pepper, to taste. Refrigerate until needed.

To make the chicken and cauliflower tikka

1   In a large bowl, stir together the yogurt, lime juice, garam masala, paprika, and salt, and generously season with pepper.

2   Add the chicken and cauliflower and toss to coat. Cover the bowl with plastic wrap. Refrigerate for at least 30 minutes or up to 6 hours.

3   Preheat the broiler. Line a sheet pan with aluminum foil.

4   Fill 4 skewers with pieces of chicken and cauliflower. You should be able to fit at least 3 pieces of each per skewer. Place the filled skewers on the prepared sheet pan.

5   Broil the skewers for 8 to 10 minutes, turning frequently with heatproof tongs to ensure even browning and cooking, until the chicken is slightly crispy, cooked through, and golden brown on all sides.

6   Remove from the oven and let rest for 2 minutes, or until the chicken registers 165°F measured at the thickest part. Serve with the cucumber raita on the side.

Gluten-Free

Grain-Free

Nut-Free

Active time:

15 minutes

Total time:

30 minutes

Ingredient tip

You can find canned chipotles in adobo in the Latin section of your grocery store. If you blend the sauce and peppers together and freeze the mixture in an ice cube tray, you can keep them around for the next time you need a smoky kick in a dish.

Chicken and Chipotle Enchilada Bake

☑ **Extra Quick** ★ **Serves 1**

This quick enchilada bake features tortillas, chicken, corn, and cheese with a smoky chipotle sauce. The result is a delicious, lasagna-like dish with tons of flavor and texture in little time.

Nonstick cooking spray

1 (14.5-ounce) can organic diced tomatoes, drained

½ canned chipotle peppers in adobo sauce

1 teaspoon adobo sauce (from the can)

1 garlic clove, peeled

Juice of 1 lime, divided

Kosher salt

Freshly ground black pepper

3 corn tortillas

1 shredded cooked chicken breast such as Garlic, Cilantro, and Lime Chicken Breasts (page 74)

½ cup frozen yellow corn kernels, thawed

½ cup shredded Monterey Jack cheese

1   Preheat the oven to 400°F. Spray a large ramekin or round ovenproof baking dish with cooking spray. Set aside.

2   In a blender, combine the tomatoes, chipotle pepper, adobo sauce, garlic, and the juice of ½ lime, and season with salt and pepper. Purée until smooth.

3   Place 2 tablespoons of the sauce in the bottom of the ramekin. Place 1 corn tortilla on top. Layer more sauce on top of the tortilla. Evenly distribute one-third of the chicken, one-third of the corn, and one-fourth of the Monterey Jack cheese over the tortilla. Top with a tortilla and cover with sauce.

4 Repeat this process with the remaining ingredients. You should end up with two filling layers stuffed between three tortillas, and a final layer of sauce and cheese on top.

5 Bake for 10 to 15 minutes, or until warmed through and the cheese is golden and melted. Top with a squeeze of lime juice from the remaining lime half and enjoy immediately.

Nut-Free

Active time:
15 minutes

Total time:
20 minutes

Variation tip
Add 1 tablespoon dried oregano and 1½ teaspoons dried rosemary to the marinade for Salt and Three Pepper Chicken Breasts (page 70) to make the chicken breasts especially Greek for this recipe.

Cooking tip
Alternatively, if you don't have a food processor, in a medium bowl, mash the beets into a paste with a potato masher and stir in the remaining ingredients.

Chicken Gyros
with Beet-ziki

☑ **Extra Quick** ⭑ **Serves 1**

With a yogurt-marinated chicken, gyros are a no-brainer for an easy, tasty dinner. Fresh greens, tomato, and a vibrant beet tzatziki sauce transform leftovers into a healthy, delicious meal.

For the beet-ziki

7 ounces all-natural canned, sliced beets, drained and rinsed

1½ cups plain low-fat Greek yogurt

1 garlic clove, minced

Juice of ½ lemon

Kosher salt

Freshly ground black pepper

2 tablespoons extra-virgin olive oil

1 cucumber, grated and squeezed of excess water

¼ cup fresh dill, chopped

For the chicken gyros

1 shredded cooked Salt and Three Pepper Chicken Breasts (page 70)

2 whole-wheat pita breads, toasted

1 tomato, sliced

½ cup baby arugula, fresh baby spinach, or watercress

½ small onion, thinly sliced (optional)

Kosher salt

Freshly ground black pepper

To make the beet-ziki

1   In a food processor, combine the beets, yogurt, garlic, lemon juice, 1 teaspoon of salt, and ½ teaspoon of pepper. Blend until the mixture is well combined and a pale pink color.

2   With the processor running slowly, add the olive oil in a thin stream. Pour the mixture into a bowl and stir in the cucumber and dill. Taste and season with salt and pepper, as needed. Set aside.

To make the chicken gyros

1   Layer the shredded chicken onto the toasted pitas.
2   Top with tomato, arugula, onion (if using), and a dollop of beet-ziki.
3   Season with salt and pepper.

Dairy-Free

Nut-Free

Active time:

15 minutes

Total time:

20 minutes

Ingredient tip

Soba are traditional Japanese noodles made from buckwheat flour. They can be served cold or warm. You can find soba in the Asian section of most grocery stores.

Chicken and Chestnut Soba Bowl

☑ *Extra Quick* ⋆ *Serves 1*

Crisp water chestnuts, meaty mushrooms, and sweet snow peas combine with chicken in a soy-sesame broth for a simple but satisfying noodle bowl.

3 ounces soba noodles (from a 9.5-ounce package)

2 cups low-sodium chicken broth

2½ tablespoons low-sodium soy sauce

¾ teaspoon ground ginger

4 ounces canned water chestnuts, drained and rinsed

4 ounces snow peas

4 ounces sliced shiitake mushrooms or oyster mushrooms

1 tablespoon tahini

1 cooked Garlic, Cilantro, and Lime Chicken Breasts (page 74), sliced

Chopped scallion, for garnish

1   Bring a large pot of water to a boil over high heat. Do not salt it. Add the soba noodles, reduce the heat to medium, and cook for no more than 5 minutes, stirring occasionally, and tasting to ensure the noodles are al dente. Drain in a colander and rinse the noodles immediately with cold water to remove the excess starch.

2   In a saucepan, bring the chicken broth to a boil over high heat.

3   Stir in the soy sauce and ginger. Lower the heat to medium.

4   Add the water chestnuts, snow peas, and mushrooms. Cook for 4 minutes.

5 In a serving bowl, combine the tahini and a ladleful of hot broth until smooth. Place the soba noodles in the sesame broth base.

6 Place the sliced chicken on top of the soba noodles. Ladle over more hot broth and vegetables. Sprinkle with the scallions.

Active time:

35 minutes

Total time:

1 hour

Ingredient tip

You can find frozen cauliflower pizza crusts with the frozen pizzas in most standard grocery stores.

Squash, Sausage, and Ricotta Cauliflower Crust Pizza

Serves 2

Similar to a fantastic pizza I ate in New York, this pie features a roasted garlic and butternut squash sauce as a base. Creamy ricotta, crumbly sausage, and peppery basil are perfect toppings.

½ butternut squash, peeled and cut into medium dice

2 garlic cloves, peeled

Extra-virgin olive oil, for drizzling

Kosher salt

Freshly ground black pepper

1 cup low-sodium vegetable broth

¾ cup heavy (whipping) cream

8 ounces ground Italian sausage

1 frozen cauliflower pizza crust, thawed

½ cup low-fat ricotta

¼ cup fresh basil, thinly sliced

1 teaspoon dried oregano

1   Preheat the oven to 450°F and position a rack in the bottom third of the oven and one in the top third. Place a sheet pan, pizza stone, or large ovenproof skillet on the bottom rack to heat. Line a large sheet pan with aluminum foil. Line a plate with paper towels and set aside.

2   Arrange the squash and garlic in a single layer on the prepared sheet pan. Drizzle with the olive oil and season with salt and pepper.

3   Roast for 20 to 25 minutes, or until the garlic is golden and squash is very tender.

4 Transfer the squash and garlic to a blender or food processor. Add the vegetable broth and cream, and season with salt and pepper. Purée for about 3 minutes, or until a smooth, thick sauce forms.

5 In a skillet over medium heat, brown the ground sausage with a drizzle of olive oil for 6 to 8 minutes, until browned, breaking it up with the back of a spoon. Using a slotted spoon, transfer the sausage to the prepared plate and set aside.

6 Place the cauliflower crust on a work surface. Spread the squash purée over the crust, leaving a 1-inch border at the edges.

7 Sprinkle the pizza with the sausage and place dollops of ricotta around the pie.

8 Sprinkle the pizza with basil. Drizzle with olive oil and season with salt and oregano.

9 Move the heated tray into the top third of the oven. Carefully transfer the pizza onto it.

10 Cook for about 10 minutes, or until the pizza crust is golden brown and crispy. Serve immediately.

Mushroom, Leek, and Asiago Cauliflower Crust Pizza

Serves 2

Mushrooms, leeks, and Asiago cheese layered on a roasted garlic cream sauce make an equally delectable (and vegetarian) alternative to the Squash, Sausage, and Ricotta Cauliflower Crust Pizza (page 86).

8 ounces sliced baby portobello or cremini mushrooms

3 garlic cloves, peeled

Extra-virgin olive oil, for drizzling

Kosher salt

Freshly ground black pepper

1 leek, halved lengthwise, washed well, and thinly sliced crosswise (light green and white parts)

1 cup low-sodium vegetable broth

¼ cup heavy (whipping) cream

6 ounces shredded Asiago cheese, divided

1 frozen cauliflower pizza crust, thawed

1 teaspoon dried oregano

1 Preheat the oven to 450°F and position a rack in the bottom third of the oven and one in the top third. Place a sheet pan, pizza stone, or large ovenproof skillet on the bottom rack to heat. Line a large sheet pan with aluminum foil.

2 Spread the mushrooms and garlic in a single layer on the prepared sheet pan. Drizzle with olive oil and season with salt and pepper.

3 Roast for 25 minutes, or until golden brown.

4 Meanwhile, place the leeks in a saucepan over medium-low heat and season with salt and pepper. Cook the leeks for about 5 minutes, or until translucent.

5   In a blender, combine the roasted garlic cloves, vegetable broth, cream, and 2 ounces of Asiago cheese. Season with salt and pepper and blend until smooth.

6   Place the pizza crust on a work surface. Spread the cream sauce over the crust, leaving a 1-inch border at the edges.

7   Distribute the mushrooms, leeks, and remaining Asiago cheese over the pizza.

8   Drizzle with olive oil and season with salt and oregano.

9   Move the heated tray into the top third of the oven. Carefully transfer the pizza onto it.

10 Cook for about 10 minutes, or until the pizza crust is golden brown and crispy. Serve immediately.

Nut-Free
Vegetarian

Active time:
15 minutes

Total time:
20 minutes

Variation tip
Substitute cauliflower for the pasta for an extra low-carb alternative. Use 8 ounces cauliflower florets, fresh or frozen, boiled for 3 minutes if frozen to thaw, or 5 to 6 minutes if fresh until tender.

One-Pan Mac and Cheese

☑ *Extra Quick* ★ *Serves 2*

This mac and cheese is the ultimate healthier comfort food. Replacing most of the milk and butter in favor of a flavored broth, cutting back slightly on the cheese, and adding nutty whole-wheat pasta makes this treat just a bit more wholesome.

2 tablespoons panko bread crumbs

4 cups water, plus more as needed

1 teaspoon kosher salt

1 teaspoon freshly ground black pepper, plus more as needed

½ teaspoon ground mustard

½ teaspoon ground paprika

8 ounces whole-wheat fusilli or rotini pasta

1 tablespoon heavy cream

½ cup shredded sharp or aged white cheddar cheese

¼ cup grated Parmesan cheese

1 In a medium saucepan over medium heat, toast the bread crumbs for about 5 minutes, or until light golden brown and crispy. Transfer to a plate and set aside.

2 In the same pan, combine the water, salt, pepper, mustard, and paprika. Place the pan over high heat and bring the water to a boil.

3 Stir in the pasta. Reduce the heat to medium-low and simmer for about 8 minutes, or until the pasta is al dente, adding more water if the water cooks off, exposing dry pasta. If liquid remains in the pan, that's okay; the pan should not be super wet but not dry.

4   Stir in the cream, then add the cheddar and Parmesan cheeses. Toss to combine. Taste and season with salt and pepper, as needed.

5   Spoon the mac and cheese into bowls and sprinkle with the bread crumbs.

Nut-Free
Vegetarian

Active time:
15 minutes

Total time:
20 minutes

Ingredient tip
Quality of ingredients is key here. Use a good block of cheese (freshly grated), freshly ground black pepper, and fresh snap peas for the best results. You'll find Pecorino-Romano near the Parmesan, and you could substitute one for the other with just a slight difference in taste.

Cacio e Pepe
with Snap Peas

☑ **Extra Quick** ☆ **Serves 2**

Meet fettucine Alfredo and spaghetti carbonara's lightened-up (and, arguably, more delicious) cousin, *cacio e pepe*. Italian for "cheese and pepper," this pasta is quick, simple, and flavorful. Quickly blanched snap peas add a burst of crunch and color.

2 tablespoons kosher salt

6 ounces whole-wheat long pasta, such as spaghetti, linguine, or bucatini

4 ounces sugar snap peas, ends removed

2 tablespoons unsalted butter

2 to 3 teaspoons freshly ground black pepper

¼ to ½ cup grated Pecorino-Romano cheese, plus more for garnish

1 Bring a large pot of salted water to a boil.

2 Add the spaghetti and cook for about 6 minutes, or until al dente. Grab the pasta with tongs and transfer to a medium bowl.

3 Add the peas to the pasta water and cook for 2 to 3 minutes, or until bright green but still crunchy. Reserve 2 cups of the pasta water before draining the peas and adding them to the pasta.

4 In a medium skillet over medium heat, melt the butter.

5 Add the pepper and cook for 2 minutes.

6 Add 1 cup of the reserved pasta water and the Pecorino-Romano cheese. Stir to combine.

7   Add the pasta and the peas to the skillet. Toss to combine with the sauce. Thin the sauce with more pasta water, as needed.

8   Plate the pasta. Sprinkle with more Pecorino-Romano cheese and season with pepper, as needed.

Nut-Free
Vegetarian

Active time:
30 minutes

Total time:
45 minutes

Cooking tip
Why cook with the pasta water? Pasta releases starch as it cooks, and starch is the secret ingredient in a sauce that sticks to the pasta. Not only that, the starchy water helps combine the butter sauce into a creamy, homogenous mixture instead of a split, oily one. Oil and water wouldn't mix without that starch.

Roasted Pepper and Artichoke Penne

Serves 3

Roasted red peppers, hearty penne, and artichokes are bathed in a lemon butter–caper sauce and baked with pockets of goat cheese for a lighter, but equally satisfying, oven-baked pasta.

Nonstick cooking spray

Kosher salt

8 ounces whole-wheat penne pasta

6 ounces roasted red peppers packed in oil, drained and quartered, 3 tablespoons oil reserved

1 tablespoon unsalted butter

1 shallot, peeled and minced

1 (14-ounce) can quartered artichoke hearts, drained, rinsed, and halved

2 tablespoons capers, drained and rinsed

Juice of 1 lemon

6 ounces goat cheese, crumbled

¼ cup basil leaves, thinly sliced

Freshly ground black pepper

1   Preheat the broiler. Coat a 9-by-13-inch baking dish with cooking spray and set aside.

2   Bring a large pot of salted water to a boil. Add the pasta and cook for 6 to 7 minutes, or until very al dente. Reserve 2 cups of pasta water and drain the pasta in a colander.

3   Heat the oil from the roasted peppers with the butter in a large sauté pan or skillet over medium-low heat, until the butter melts.

4   Add the shallot. Sauté for 4 to 5 minutes, or until the shallot is nearly dissolved and fragrant.

5   Stir in the roasted red peppers and artichoke hearts. Cook for 2 to 3 minutes.

6   Add the capers and lemon juice. Toss to combine.

7   Add the pasta to the pan and toss to coat it in the sauce. Thin the sauce with reserved pasta water, as needed, to create a creamy consistency. Cook for 1 to 2 minutes.

8   Fold in half the goat cheese and the basil. Pour the pasta mixture into the prepared baking dish and dot the top with the remaining cheese.

9   Broil the pasta for 4 to 6 minutes, or until slightly crispy around the edges and the goat cheese is golden and bubbly. Remove from the oven and cool slightly before serving.

Active time:

35 minutes

Total time:

40 minutes

Cooking tip

If you're in a hurry, microwave the squash. Cook the halves in the microwave for 12 to 15 minutes on high power, in 5-minute increments, until fork-tender. If you don't have a food processor, chop the ingredients by hand and stir them together in a bowl.

Spaghetti Squash
with Tomatoes and Olives

Serves 2

At first glance, it's hard to tell this squash is, well, squash. A low-carb alternative to pasta, this spaghetti squash roasts in the oven and is tossed with a fresh blend of tomatoes and olives to cut through some of its sweetness. This makes a great main dish as well as a side.

1 medium spaghetti squash, halved lengthwise, seeds and pulp removed with a spoon

1 tablespoon extra-virgin olive oil, plus more for the squash

Kosher salt

Freshly ground black pepper

1 cup pitted Kalamata olives

1 cup packaged sun-dried tomatoes (not packed in oil)

2 tablespoons capers, drained

2 garlic cloves, crushed

¼ cup fresh flat-leaf Italian parsley, chopped

Crumbled feta cheese, for topping (optional)

1 Preheat the oven to 400°F. Line a sheet pan with aluminum foil.

2 Drizzle each spaghetti squash half with olive oil and generously season with salt and pepper. Place the halves, cut-side down, on the prepared sheet pan.

3 Roast the spaghetti squash for 30 minutes, or until the flesh is fork-tender. Remove the squash from the oven and let cool for 1 to 2 minutes.

4 Meanwhile, in a food processor, combine the olives, sun-dried tomatoes, capers, garlic, and parsley. Season with salt and pepper. Pulse the mixture for 1 minute.

5 Add the olive oil and pulse to combine. The final spread should be relatively smooth with some texture, not a creamy paste.

6 Using a fork (and an oven mitt for protection), scrape the flesh of each spaghetti squash half into a bowl. Mix with half the tomato-olive mixture. Season with salt and pepper, as needed.

7 Pile the spaghetti squash on a serving plate and top with the remaining tomato-olive mixture and feta cheese (if using).

Gluten-Free

Grain-Free

Nut-Free

Vegetarian

Active time:

20 minutes

Total time:

25 minutes

Variation tip

You could also spoon the filling, beans, cheese, and avocado into hard and soft tortillas for tacos.

Sweet Potato, Black Bean, and Avocado Quesadillas

☑ Extra Quick ⭐ Serves 2

A smoky sweet potato mash, black beans, and creamy avocado make a great replacement for cheese and meat in these quesadillas. Broiling them rather than panfrying keeps them healthier than your typical cheese-and-flour melt.

Nonstick cooking spray

1 sweet potato

1½ teaspoons chili powder

1 teaspoon ground cinnamon

½ teaspoon dried oregano

¼ cup reduced-fat sour cream, plus more for serving

1 avocado, halved and pitted (see tip, page 19)

4 corn tortillas

¾ (15-ounce) can black beans, drained and rinsed

2 ounces queso fresco, crumbled

1 Preheat the broiler. Line a sheet pan with aluminum foil and coat the foil with cooking spray. Set aside.

2 Poke the sweet potato all over with a fork. Microwave it for 5 minutes on high power, then in 30-second increments until the skin has puffed up slightly and the potato flesh is fork-tender. Let cool for 3 minutes.

3 Scoop the sweet potato flesh into a medium bowl. Using a fork, mash it just until smooth. Stir in the chili powder, cinnamon, and oregano. Fold in the sour cream. Set aside.

4 Using a spoon, scoop the avocado flesh out of the skins and thinly slice it. Set aside.

5   Place the tortillas on a work surface. On one tortilla, spread half of the mashed sweet potato. Top with half each of the avocado, black beans, and queso fresco. Top with the other corn tortilla and press down to flatten slightly. Repeat with the remaining ingredients for a second quesadilla. Place the quesadillas on the prepared sheet pan.

6   Broil for 2 minutes per side, or until the exterior is golden brown and crispy. Let cool for 1 to 2 minutes.

7   Using a serrated knife, cut each quesadilla into thirds.

Gluten-Free

Grain-Free

Vegan

Active time:

20 minutes

Total time:

30 minutes

Ingredient tip

Pressing tofu of excess moisture ensures you don't end up with a watery dish, and your tofu is firmer while cooking. To press tofu of excess water, wrap the drained block in a layer of paper towels and place it on a plate. Place another plate on top of the tofu and add a heavy can or other weighted object to the top plate. Let sit for about 10 minutes. Remove the weights, unwrap the tofu, and prepare as directed.

Tofu, Broccoli, and Peanut Sauté

☑ *Extra Quick* ★ *Serves 1*

This sauté is simple but far from boring with its Afro-Indian-inspired peanut sauce. Tofu soaks up all the lovely flavors of peanut and coconut. Although tomato paste may seem unusual in this context, it adds a certain acidity that rounds out the rich peanut butter and coconut milk.

4 ounces coconut milk

2 tablespoons creamy peanut butter

1½ teaspoons tomato paste

½ teaspoon ground ginger

¼ teaspoon cayenne pepper, plus more as needed

1 tablespoon coconut oil

½ (14-ounce) block extra-firm tofu, drained, dried, and pressed of excess water (see tip), cut into 1-inch cubes

½ head broccoli, stems peeled and cut into 1-inch cubes, head cut into florets

5 ounces canned baby corn, drained and rinsed

¼ cup water

1   In a small saucepan over medium-low heat, stir together the coconut milk, peanut butter, tomato paste, ginger, and cayenne pepper. Heat for 5 to 6 minutes, or until warm and well mixed. Remove from heat and set aside.

2 Heat the coconut oil in a medium skillet over medium-high heat. Add the tofu and sauté for about 4 minutes until colored on all sides. Add the broccoli and baby corn to the skillet and sauté for 5 to 6 minutes more, or until the broccoli stems begin to soften.

3 Add the water, cover the skillet, and steam for 2 minutes.

4 Toss the tofu and veggies with the peanut sauce to serve.

Active time:

25 minutes

Total time:

30 minutes

Ingredient tip

Look for Vietnamese rice paper wraps in the Asian section of most grocery stores, or by the sushi counter. It's actually better, when working with them, to under-soak them slightly than to wait until they are completely limp before filling. The wraps, once moistened, will continue to soften on the board.

Variation tip

If you prefer, enjoy the filling as a salad with the mango sauce as a dressing.

Summer Rolls
with Mango-Sriracha Sauce

☑ **Extra Quick** ★ **Serves 2**

Light and refreshing summer rolls with red bell pepper, carrot, cucumber, cabbage, and herbs make a beautiful and practical salad wrap. A quick mango-Sriracha dipping sauce adds some sweet heat without a ton of added sugar, which can be found in many bottled sweet chili sauces. These wraps are vegan, but they can also be made with meat and seafood.

½ head Napa cabbage, ribs removed, and leaves cut into thin strips

¼ cup fresh basil leaves

¼ cup fresh mint leaves

2 carrots, cut into thin strips using a vegetable peeler

1 cucumber, peeled and cut into thin strips

1 red bell pepper, seeded and cut into thin strips

6 Vietnamese (8-inch diameter) rice paper wrappers

4 ounces rice vermicelli noodles, prepared according to the package directions, rinsed with cool water and drained

1 mango, peeled, pitted, and diced

½ cup water

1 teaspoon Sriracha, or more, to taste

1 In a medium bowl, gently toss cabbage with basil and mint.

2 On a sheet tray lined with parchment paper, carefully arrange piles of the cabbage mixture, carrot, cucumber, and red bell pepper.

3 Fill a large shallow bowl with lukewarm water. Carefully dip all edges of a rice paper wrap into the water for no more than 5 seconds per side (see tip). Remove and place the wrap on a work surface.

4   Lay one-fourth of the rice noodles on the bottom third of the wrap followed by one-fourth of the cabbage mixture. Place 2 strips each of carrot, cucumber, and red pepper on top. Fold the bottom edge of the rice wrap over the filling (it should be well stuffed). Then fold in the sides of the wrap and roll up. Set aside and repeat with the remaining wraps and ingredients.

5   In a blender, combine the mango and water. Purée until smooth. Pour the sauce into a small serving bowl and stir in the Sriracha.

6   Serve the wraps with the sauce immediately, or refrigerate for up to 1 hour.

Nut-Free
Vegetarian

Active time:
40 minutes

Total time:
45 minutes

Ingredient tip
Consider using this mushroom technique (see steps 2 and 3) as a stand-in for other meat dishes and sandwiches, such as pulled pork or chicken. Some mushrooms, such as king oysters, are even used as a substitute for seafood, like scallops.

Pulled Portobello Panini

Serves 1

This tasty vegetarian sandwich features delicious shredded and roasted portobello mushrooms. Horseradish mayo and red onion offer some zing, and arugula adds a peppery kick.

4 ounces portobello mushrooms

½ teaspoon kosher salt, plus more as needed

1 teaspoon freshly ground black pepper, plus more as needed

¾ teaspoon garlic powder

½ teaspoon paprika

3 tablespoons extra-virgin olive oil

2 tablespoons light mayonnaise

1½ teaspoons prepared horseradish

½ French baguette, halved lengthwise

2 ounces sharp white cheddar cheese, sliced

¼ red onion, thinly sliced

¼ cup baby arugula

1　Preheat the oven to 350°F. Line a sheet pan with aluminum foil.

2　Remove the stems from the mushroom caps. Remove the dirty parts of the stems, then use two forks to shred the stems into strands. Thinly slice the mushroom caps and roughly chop those slices into more thin strands. Place the mushrooms on the prepared sheet pan and season them with salt, pepper, garlic powder, paprika. Drizzle olive oil over the mushrooms. Toss to coat and spread into a single layer.

3　Roast for 30 minutes until meaty, tender, and a rich brown color. Set aside to cool.

4　In a small bowl, stir together the mayonnaise and horseradish. Spread the mixture onto the cut sides of the baguette halves.

5 On one baguette half, layer on the cheddar cheese, red onion, mushrooms, and arugula. Close the sandwich.

6 In a panini press on medium-high heat, cook the sandwich for 4 to 5 minutes, or until the cheese melts and the bread crisps. Alternatively, broil the sandwich, open-faced without the greens, for 4 minutes. Then add the greens, close, and serve.

Active time:
35 minutes

Total time:
40 minutes

Cooking tip
What's the secret to perfectly cooked rice? For one, the water-to-rice ratio, which can vary depending on the type of rice, and which is usually 1 part rice to 1½ parts water (or other liquid). If the rice starts to look dry before it's done, add a bit more water to keep it from burning. The other key is patience. Once you've lowered the heat to a simmer, cover the pan and leave it be. When it's done, let it sit for a few minutes. Do not fluff the rice until just before using it, and do so with a fork. And, if you really want that floral note of the jasmine in your jasmine rice, consider soaking your rice for about 15 minutes before draining, rinsing, and cooking.

Pineapple-Cashew Fried Rice
with Shrimp

Serves 3

Inspired by a favorite dish from the Thai restaurant down the street, this stir-fried, curried jasmine rice with shrimp, pepper, eggs, pineapple, and cashews makes a delicious and filling meal.

1¾ cups water

1 cup jasmine rice, rinsed and drained

2 tablespoons coconut oil

4 ounces peeled and deveined jumbo shrimp

2 large eggs, beaten

½ red bell pepper, cut into matchsticks

½ cup cashews, chopped

1 (8-ounce) can pineapple chunks in juice, drained

¼ cup coconut milk

2 teaspoons yellow curry powder

Kosher salt

1 In a medium saucepan over high heat, bring the water and rice to a boil. Reduce the heat to low, cover the pan, and simmer for 20 minutes, or until all the water is absorbed and the rice is cooked.

2 Heat the coconut oil in a medium skillet over medium heat. Add the shrimp and sauté for about 5 minutes until they are rosy, opaque, and curled. Remove from the pan and set aside.

3 Return the skillet to medium heat and add the eggs. Cook for 2 to 3 minutes, stirring.

4   Add the red bell pepper and cashews and sauté for 3 to 4 minutes, or until the pepper begins to soften and the cashews are toasted.

5   Stir in the rice and pineapple, then add the shrimp and stir to combine.

6   Stir in the coconut milk, curry powder, and salt to taste. Cook for 1 minute more.

Active time:
20 minutes

Total time:
1 hour

Cooking tip
When cooking pork chops, look for a nice golden crust on each side—which can be achieved by leaving the chop alone when cooking, not flipping it too much—and a slightly rosy interior. If you have achieved all of these, congratulations, you cooked a pork chop to perfection! Marinate the meat a day in advance and you'll reduce the prep time for this meal.

Korean-Inspired Pork Chop
with Cucumber Salad

Serves 1

A Korean-style marinade amps up the umami flavor on this simple pork chop. Warm plays off cold with a slightly spicy cucumber and bean sprout topping.

4 tablespoons low-sodium soy sauce, divided

2 tablespoons sesame oil

3 tablespoons light brown sugar, divided

2 garlic cloves, minced

⅓ Asian pear or Fuji apple, grated

Freshly ground black pepper

1 (1-inch-thick) bone-in pork chop

2 tablespoons rice wine vinegar

Red pepper flakes, for seasoning

⅓ cucumber, thinly sliced

⅓ cup bean sprouts

1 In a medium bowl, stir together 2 tablespoons of soy sauce, the sesame oil, 2 tablespoons of brown sugar, the garlic, and the pear. Season with pepper and stir to combine. Submerge the pork chop in the marinade. Cover the bowl with plastic wrap and refrigerate for at least 30 minutes or up to 24 hours.

2 In a small bowl, whisk the remaining 2 tablespoons of soy sauce, 1 tablespoon of brown sugar, and vinegar. Season with red pepper flakes and whisk to combine. Stir in the cucumber and bean sprouts. Set aside.

3 Bring the pork chop to room temperature and remove any excess marinade from it. Discard leftover marinade.

4 Place a skillet or grill pan over medium-high heat.

5 Add the chop and cook for 6 to 7 minutes per side. Using tongs, render the white strip of fat along the back of the chop by searing that side for 2 to 3 minutes. Check that the internal temperature of the thickest part of the chop registers just below 145°F measured on an instant-read thermometer.

6 Remove pork chop to a plate, and let rest for about 5 minutes before serving with the cucumber bean sprouts salad.

Dairy-Free
Gluten-Free
Grain-Free
Nut-Free

Active time:
25 minutes

Total time:
40 minutes

Ingredient tip
Ancho chili powder is made of dried and ground poblano peppers. It is one of the milder chili pepper products and it can be found with the spices in many grocery stores. Ask your fishmonger to remove the pin bones for you. If you do it yourself, use a sterile pair of tweezers and hold down the flesh around the bone as you pull them out.

Ancho and Agave Salmon
with Zucchini

Serves 2

A smoky and sweet spice crust on baked salmon with caramelized zucchini combine for a simple and delicious sheet pan dinner.

3 zucchini, cut into medium dice

2 tablespoons extra-virgin olive oil

Kosher salt

Freshly ground black pepper

1 tablespoon agave nectar

1½ teaspoons ancho chili powder

1 teaspoon ground cumin

½ teaspoon garlic powder

2 skin-on medium salmon fillets, or 1 large fillet, pin bones removed, at room temperature

1 lime, halved

¼ cup fresh cilantro, chopped

1 Preheat the oven to 400°F. Line a sheet pan with aluminum foil.

2 On the prepared sheet pan, arrange the zucchini in a single layer. Drizzle with olive oil and season with salt and pepper. Toss to coat.

3 Roast for 15 minutes.

4 Meanwhile, in a small bowl, stir together the agave nectar, ancho chili powder, cumin, and garlic powder until a thin paste forms. Season with salt and pepper and stir to combine.

5 Place the salmon fillets on a plate, skin-side down. Coat the flesh with the ancho chili rub. Set aside for 5 minutes.

6 Move the zucchini to one side of the sheet pan, and stir it. Place the salmon fillets, skin-side down, on the other side of the pan.

7   Bake for 8 to 10 minutes, or until the fish's internal temperature registers 145°F. Remove from the oven and let rest for 2 to 3 minutes.

8   Squeeze the juice of ½ lime over the salmon and the remaining ½ lime over the zucchini. Top with the cilantro.

5

FAMILY DINNER

Nut-Free

Active time:
35 minutes

Total time:
40 minutes

Cooking tip

To dredge means to coat all sides of an ingredient in a powdered mixture, usually seasoned flour—or in this case, baking powder. I find it's easiest to lay the item to be dredged in the dredging mixture and then pile the dredging mixture all over it to evenly coat. Cooking the wings on a rack, lifted away from the sheet pan, helps crisp the wings on all sides and prevents a soggy bottom.

Apricot-Soy Baked Chicken Wings

Serves 4

A seasoned baking powder coating makes these baked wings as crispy as their deep-fried counterparts with very little fat. Sweet, salty, and spicy apricot glaze replaces the traditional Buffalo sauce.

2 tablespoons baking powder

2 teaspoons garlic powder

1 teaspoon paprika

Kosher salt

Freshly ground black pepper

2 pounds chicken wings, at room temperature

½ cup apricot preserves

2 tablespoons unsalted butter

1½ tablespoons low-sodium soy sauce

1 tablespoon Dijon mustard

1 Preheat the oven to 425°F. Line two sheet pans with aluminum foil and place a wire rack on top of each.

2 In a large bowl, stir together the baking powder, garlic powder, and paprika, and season with salt and pepper. Dredge (see tip) the wings in the mixture and place them on the prepared rack.

3 Bake for 30 minutes, turning frequently, until crispy and golden brown. Remove from the oven and set aside.

4 Meanwhile, in a small microwave-safe bowl, stir together the apricot preserves, butter, soy sauce, and mustard. Microwave on high for 2 to 3 minutes, or until hot and bubbly, and stir. Season with salt and pepper, as needed, and stir once more.

5 In a large bowl, combine the crispy wings and apricot glaze. Toss to coat.

Baja Turkey Burgers

☑ Extra Quick ⭐ **Serves 4**

Smoky chipotle turkey burgers, creamy Monterey Jack cheese, and quick-pickled red onion star in this Southwestern burger. Replacing the traditional condiments with mashed avocado keeps things creamy and tasty with healthier fats in the mix.

1 pound ground turkey

1 canned chipotle pepper in adobo sauce, chopped finely

1 tablespoon adobo sauce (from the can)

1 teaspoon ground cumin

1½ teaspoons kosher salt, divided, plus more as needed

1 teaspoon freshly ground black pepper, plus more as needed

½ red onion, thinly sliced

2 tablespoons white wine vinegar

1 tablespoon agave nectar

Nonstick cooking spray

4 ounces Monterey Jack cheese, shredded

1 avocado, halved, pitted (see tip, page 19)

4 burger buns, halved and toasted

½ head iceberg lettuce, shredded

1 In a medium bowl, combine the ground turkey, chipotle chili, adobo sauce, cumin, 1 teaspoon of salt, and pepper. Mix to combine. Divide the turkey mixture into 4 portions and shape each into a patty. Use your thumb to make a dimple in the center of each patty. Place the formed patties on a plate and chill for at least 5 minutes.

2 In a small bowl, combine the red onion, vinegar, and agave. Let the onion sit to marinate for at least 10 minutes.

3 Lightly coat a grill, grill pan, or skillet with cooking spray and preheat it to medium-high heat.

Continued ▶

Nut-Free

🕐

Active time:
20 minutes

Total time:
25 minutes

Cooking tip
Do not press down on the burgers while cooking. Leave them be. The dimple in each burger will keep them flat on the grill, and not applying extra pressure will keep more juices inside the meat.

Baja Turkey Burgers Continued

4 Place the burgers on the grill and cook for 4 to 5 minutes per side, or until golden brown and cooked through.

5 Top each burger with one-fourth of the cheese and let it melt. Transfer the burgers to a clean plate and let rest for 2 minutes.

6 Scoop the avocado flesh into a small bowl and add the remaining ½ teaspoon of salt. Using a fork, mash the avocado and salt to combine.

7 Spread the mashed avocado on both halves of the toasted rolls. Top the bottom roll with a burger, quick-pickled red onion, and shredded iceberg lettuce. Close the sandwiches and serve.

Grilled Shrimp and Melon Skewers

Serves 4

A quick honey-lime grilling sauce makes these sweet and fresh shrimp and melon skewers perfect for a summertime barbecue. You'll need to soak 8 bamboo or wooden skewers in water for at least 1 hour before grilling.

1 medium cantaloupe, halved and seeded

1 medium honeydew melon, halved and seeded

1 pound peeled and deveined jumbo shrimp

¼ cup honey

Juice of 2 limes

2 tablespoons low-sodium soy sauce

Nonstick cooking spray

½ cup toasted walnuts, chopped

1. Cut each half of the cantaloupe and honeydew in half, then cut off the skin from each quarter. Cut the melon into cubes.
2. Build the skewers by alternating shrimp, cantaloupe, and honeydew.
3. In a small bowl, stir together the honey, lime juice, and soy sauce.
4. Coat a grill, grill pan, or skillet with cooking spray and preheat it to medium heat.
5. Grill the skewers on all sides, basting with the sauce, for 5 to 6 minutes, or until the melon is slightly caramelized and shrimp are pink and opaque.
6. Sprinkle with the walnuts and serve.

Dairy-Free

Active time:
15 minutes

Total time:
1 hour, 20 minutes

Cooking tip
Don't overfill or underfill your skewers with food. This is often what contributes to food sliding off the skewers.

Dairy-Free
Gluten-Free
Nut-Free

Active time:
40 minutes

Total time:
1 hour

Ingredient tip
If you cannot find andouille sausage, substitute any smoked sausage and increase the amount of Cajun seasoning. You could also shred some leftover Salt and Three Pepper Chicken Breasts (page 70), if you have it on hand, and mix it into this jambalaya.

Sausage and Shrimp Jambalaya

Serves 4

This simple Cajun-style classic takes me back to the few days I spent exploring the French Quarter with family and friends. Jambalaya is straightforward, flavorful, and filling. Sausage and shrimp are the stars in this version.

8 ounces andouille sausage, removed from its casings, cut into medium dice

1 bunch celery, cut into medium dice

2 green bell peppers, seeded and cut into medium dice

1 onion, cut into medium dice

Kosher salt

Freshly ground black pepper

1 cup long-grain white rice, rinsed and drained

1 (15-ounce) can organic diced tomatoes with their juice

2 cups low-sodium chicken broth, warmed

1 bay leaf

2¼ teaspoons Cajun seasoning, plus more as needed

8 ounces peeled and deveined jumbo shrimp

1   In a large pot or Dutch oven over medium-high heat, cook the sausage for 4 to 5 minutes, or until browned and crispy. Using a slotted spoon, remove the sausage from the pot, but leave the fat behind.

2   Add the celery, green bell peppers, and onion to the rendered sausage fat and season with salt and pepper. Sauté for about 5 minutes, or until the onion starts to become translucent and the veggies soften slightly.

3   Add the rice to the pot and stir to combine. Toast for 1 minute.

4 Add the tomatoes with juice and chicken broth to deglaze the pot, stirring with a wooden spoon to loosen any browned bits stuck to the bottom.

5 Stir in the browned sausage, bay leaf, and Cajun seasoning. Bring the mixture to a boil. Reduce the heat to medium-low, cover the pot, and simmer for 20 to 25 minutes, or until the liquid is mostly absorbed.

6 Remove the lid, add the shrimp, and cook for 5 minutes, or until the shrimp are pink, cooked, and curled slightly. Stir to incorporate.

7 Remove and discard the bay leaf. Taste and add more Cajun seasoning, salt, and pepper, as needed.

Active time:

30 minutes

Total time:

50 minutes

Variation tip

Substitute frozen spinach, thawed and squeezed of excess moisture, for the broccoli. A variety of grains—from rice pilaf to brown rice to farro—can be used.

Barley, Ricotta, and Broccoli Casserole

Serves 8 to 10

Creamy cheese, hearty barley, and chopped broccoli create a comforting and filling casserole, or *gratin*, which is a French dish (often of vegetables) baked with cheese or bread crumbs on top to form a brown crust.

Nonstick cooking spray

1 (11-ounce) box pearled, quick cooking barley

½ cup water

2 (10-ounce) boxes frozen chopped broccoli

1 (32-ounce) container fat-free or reduced-fat ricotta

1 cup shredded mozzarella cheese

½ cup shredded Parmesan cheese, plus more for topping

2 large eggs

½ teaspoon ground nutmeg

Kosher salt

Freshly ground black pepper

1 Preheat the oven to 350°F. Lightly coat a 9-by-13-inch baking dish with cooking spray. Set aside.

2 Cook the barley according to package directions. Pour it into the prepared baking dish.

3 While the barley cooks, combine the water and frozen broccoli in a medium sauté pan or skillet over medium heat. Cook for 8 minutes.

4 In a large bowl, stir together the ricotta, mozzarella cheese, Parmesan cheese, eggs, and nutmeg, and season with salt and pepper.

5 Layer the broccoli over the barley.

6   Spread the cheese mixture evenly over the top. Sprinkle with more Parmesan cheese and season with pepper.
7   Bake for 25 minutes, or until the cheese layer is set and the Parmesan top is crispy and golden brown.

Nut-Free
Vegetarian

Active time:
25 minutes

Total time:
40 minutes

Cooking tip
To remove thyme leaves, hold the stem by the top with one hand. Pinch your thumb and forefinger of the other hand near where you're holding it and run your fingers against the leaves down the stem until you reach the bottom. The leaves will come off easily. Pick off the remaining few leaves at the top. This technique also works well with rosemary.

Twice-Baked Sweet Potatoes

Serves 4

These twice-baked sweet potatoes have a bit of an Italian twist with mascarpone and Pecorino-Romano cheeses. The maple brown butter with fresh thyme takes these to the next level. Perfect for the holiday season, these potatoes are worth the extra effort because of their crispy top and creamy interior.

2 medium sweet potatoes

2 tablespoons mascarpone, ricotta, or reduced-fat cream cheese, at room temperature

Grated zest of ½ orange

1 teaspoon ground nutmeg

¼ teaspoon kosher salt, plus more as needed

Freshly ground black pepper

Grated Pecorino-Romano cheese, for topping

2 tablespoons unsalted butter

1 tablespoon pure maple syrup

4 thyme sprigs, leaves removed and chopped

1 Poke the sweet potatoes all over with a fork. Microwave for 5 minutes on high power, then in 30-second increments until the potatoes are cooked and fork-tender. Set aside for 1 to 2 minutes before handling.

2 Preheat the oven to 375°F. Line a sheet pan with aluminum foil and set aside.

3 Halve the sweet potatoes while still warm. Using a spoon, scoop their flesh into a medium bowl, leaving some of the sweet potato flesh inside the shell for support. Mash the scooped-out flesh with a fork.

4   Stir in the mascarpone, orange zest, nutmeg, and salt, and season with pepper. Divide the mixture evenly among the sweet potato shells and top each with Pecorino-Romano cheese. Place the stuffed sweet potato halves on the prepared sheet pan.

5   Bake for 15 to 20 minutes, or until warmed through and the cheese is golden brown and crispy on top.

6   Meanwhile, in a small saucepan over medium heat, melt the butter and cook it for about 5 minutes, or until the milk solids start to brown and the butter smells nutty. Turn off the heat immediately, and stir in an ice cube to stop the cooking. Stir in the maple syrup and thyme. Set aside.

7   Serve the sweet potatoes drizzled with the maple thyme butter.

Gluten-Free
Grain-Free
Nut-Free
Vegan

Active time:
15 minutes

Total time:
25 minutes

Ingredient tip
Prepare this spice rub in advance and keep it on hand for seasoning other proteins, vegan or not. It's especially good on beef.

Coffee-Rubbed Tofu

☑ *Extra Quick* ★ *Serves 4*

Definitely not your average Joe recipe. Steak is seasoned with coffee all the time, so why not apply this sweet, savory, smoky rub to tofu? This dry-rubbed meat substitute is perfect for a summer barbecue.

Nonstick cooking spray

2 tablespoons light brown sugar

1 tablespoon finely ground espresso powder

2 teaspoons ancho chili powder

1½ teaspoons freshly ground black pepper

1 teaspoon kosher salt

½ teaspoon paprika

1 (16-ounce) block extra-firm tofu, drained, dried, and pressed (see tip, page 100), cut into 8 long slabs

1 Coat a grill, grill pan, or skillet with cooking spray and preheat it to medium heat.
2 In a small bowl, stir together the brown sugar, espresso powder, ancho chili powder, pepper, salt, and paprika.
3 Generously season the tofu slabs on all sides with the spice rub. Let sit for 15 minutes.
4 Place the tofu planks on the grill and cook for about 3 minutes per side, or until warmed through.

Pineapple Teriyaki Chick'un

Serves 4

Teriyaki—a quick Japanese marinade of soy sauce, rice wine, and sugar—gets a tropical meatless twist. The enzymes in the pineapple juice tenderize the protein and make a sweet, fruity sauce that is perfect in the summer.

¼ cup pineapple juice

¼ cup low-sodium soy sauce

¼ cup packed dark brown sugar

2 garlic cloves, minced

1 (1-inch) piece fresh ginger, peeled and grated

8 ounces tofu, tempeh, seitan, or frozen chicken substitute protein, cut into 12 long planks

Nonstick cooking spray

2 tablespoons sliced scallion

1   In a small bowl, whisk the pineapple juice, soy sauce, brown sugar, garlic, and ginger until combined.

2   In a gallon-size resealable plastic bag, combine the tofu and marinade. Seal the bag and refrigerate for at least 30 minutes or up to 24 hours.

3   Coat a grill, grill pan, or skillet with cooking spray and preheat it to medium heat.

4   Bring the tofu to room temperature, then remove it from the marinade. Transfer the excess marinade to a small saucepan.

Continued ▸

Nut-Free
Vegan

🕐

Active time:
15 minutes

Total time:
1 hour

Ingredient tip
Look for tofu, tempeh, and frozen chicken substitute proteins in the produce and frozen sections of most grocery stores. Seitan can be found at health food stores or specialty stores such as Whole Foods.

Pineapple Teriyaki Chick'un Continued

5 Grill the tofu for about 3 minutes per side, or until a caramelized crust forms on each side. Remove and set aside.

6 Bring the remaining marinade to a boil over high heat, then reduce the heat to low and simmer for 10 to 15 minutes, or until thick and glossy.

7 Serve the tofu with the sauce spooned over the top.

Mediterranean Mushroom Caps

Serves 4

Meaty mushroom caps are filled with a Mediterranean quinoa stuffing made with tomatoes, olives, chickpeas, and hearts of palm. Serve this as a main dish with a dollop of Greek yogurt or maybe some leftover Beet-ziki (page 82).

Nonstick cooking spray

⅓ cup dried quinoa, rinsed well and drained

½ (15-ounce) can all-natural chickpeas, drained and rinsed

⅓ cup feta cheese, crumbled

4 ounces hearts of palm, drained, rinsed, and sliced

⅓ cup sun-dried tomatoes, chopped

1 (2.5-ounce) can sliced, pitted black olives, drained and rinsed

¼ cup fresh dill, roughly chopped

Freshly ground black pepper

4 large portobello mushroom caps, stemmed

2 tablespoons extra-virgin olive oil

Kosher salt

1 Preheat the oven to 375°F. Line a sheet pan with aluminum foil and coat it with cooking spray. Set aside.

2 Cook the quinoa according to the package directions.

Gluten-Free
Nut-Free
Vegetarian

Active time:
30 minutes

Total time:
40 minutes

Cooking tip
The key when using canned goods in your healthy cooking plan is to choose products that are all natural, and always drain and rinse your canned products before using them. That helps get rid of any canned taste and additives.

Continued ▶

Mediterranean Mushroom Caps Continued

3   In a medium bowl, combine the quinoa, chickpeas, feta cheese, hearts of palm, sun-dried tomatoes, olives, and dill, and season with pepper. Fill each mushroom cap with the mixture. Place the mushroom caps on the prepared sheet pan. Drizzle with olive oil and season with salt and pepper.

4   Bake for 20 to 25 minutes, or until the filling is golden brown on top and the mushrooms are tender.

Lentil and Chickpea Burgers

Serves 6

Middle Eastern-spiced and gluten-free, these protein-packed burgers come together quickly and taste as delicious as their meaty cousins. Serve on a toasted bun with the fixings of your choice.

1 cup dried green or brown lentils, rinsed, drained, and picked through for stones or debris

3 cups water

1 (15-ounce) can all-natural chickpeas, drained and rinsed

2 tablespoons extra-virgin olive oil

2 garlic cloves, minced

1½ teaspoons ground coriander

1½ teaspoons kosher salt, plus more as needed

1 teaspoon ground cumin

1 teaspoon paprika

1 teaspoon freshly ground black pepper

½ teaspoon caraway seeds

⅓ cup steel cut oats, ground

Nonstick cooking spray

Gluten-Free

Nut-Free

Vegan

Active time:
30 minutes

Total time:
40 minutes

Cooking tip
To make oat flour or ground oats, pulverize the oats in a food processor. Oat flour may also be available pre-ground with the non-wheat flours in your grocery store. The burger mixture can also be made in a food processor.

1. In a small saucepan over high heat, combine the lentils and water. Bring to a boil. Reduce the heat to a simmer and cook the lentils for 10 to 12 minutes, or until soft but not mushy. Drain any excess water and pour the lentils into a medium bowl.
2. Add the chickpeas, olive oil, garlic, coriander, salt, cumin, paprika, pepper, and caraway seeds. Using a fork or potato masher, mash the mixture until a rough paste forms, no more than 4 minutes.
3. Fold in the oats until a thick mixture forms; it should hold together when pressed.

Continued ▶

Lentil and Chickpea Burgers Continued

4 Form the lentil mixture into 6 patties, slightly more than ½-inch thick. Use your thumb to press a dimple into the center of each patty. Place formed patties onto a plate, and refrigerate for at least 5 minutes to firm up.

5 Generously coat a grill, grill pan, or skillet with cooking spray and preheat it to medium-high heat.

6 Grill the patties for 3 to 4 minutes per side. Serve as desired.

Stuffed Peppers
with Tomatoes and Black Beans

Serves 8

Cubanelle peppers are mild green oblong peppers that are a great change of pace for stuffing instead of bell peppers. This recipe is adapted from a family recipe and features a Mexican cheese-and-rice stuffing with stewed tomatoes and beans. For all your effort, the peppers are ready relatively quickly.

8 ounces yellow saffron rice

4 ounces shredded Mexican cheese blend

2 tablespoons all-purpose flour

1½ teaspoons dried oregano

1 teaspoon garlic powder

½ teaspoon ground cumin

Kosher salt

Freshly ground black pepper

1 (28-ounce) can organic diced tomatoes with their juice

1 (15-ounce) can black beans, drained and rinsed

8 Cubanelle (Italian frying) peppers, tops cut off and reserved, seeded

Reduced fat sour cream, for serving

1 Preheat the oven to 350°F.

2 Cook the rice according to the package directions.

3 In a small bowl, toss together the Mexican cheese and flour.

4 In a large bowl, stir together the cooked rice, oregano, garlic powder, and cumin, and season with salt and pepper. Add the flour-coated cheese and stir to combine.

Continued ▶

Gluten-Free

Nut-Free

Vegetarian

Active time:
40 minutes

Total time:
45 minutes

Ingredient tip
If you can't find Cubanelle peppers, also known as Italian frying peppers, use either green bell peppers or poblano chilies.

5   Pour the tomatoes and beans into a 9-by-13-inch baking dish.

6   Stuff the peppers with the cheese and rice mixture, but do not overstuff them. Lay the peppers in the baking dish and carefully cap with the reserved pepper tops to keep the filling inside.

7   Bake for 25 minutes, basting the peppers with the tomatoes and beans occasionally, until the peppers are tender.

8   Serve a pepper with some of the tomatoes and black beans spooned over the top with a dollop of sour cream.

Baked Samosa Cups

Serves 6

Indian street food staple meets American country classic in these samosa cups filled with curried peas and potatoes. Tortillas make assembly easy, and baking cuts the fat for a lighter but flavorful entrée.

Nonstick cooking spray

1 tablespoon coconut oil

4 to 6 Yukon Gold potatoes, peeled and cut into medium dice

½ onion, cut into medium dice

2 garlic cloves, minced

1 cup frozen peas

1 tablespoon tomato paste

1½ cups coconut milk

1 tablespoon yellow curry powder

Kosher salt

Freshly ground black pepper

12 white corn tortillas

1 Preheat the oven to 350°F and position a rack in the center. Coat a standard muffin tin with cooking spray and set aside.

2 Heat the coconut oil in a medium skillet over medium heat.

3 Add the potatoes, onion, and garlic. Sauté for 5 to 6 minutes, or until the potatoes develop a little color and start to soften.

4 Stir in the peas and tomato paste. Sauté for 2 minutes.

5 Add the coconut milk and curry powder and season with salt and pepper. Simmer for 5 minutes. Using a fork or potato masher, mash the mixture into a textured purée.

Continued ▶

Dairy-Free
Nut-Free
Vegetarian

Active time:
30 minutes

Total time:
45 minutes

■
Make-ahead tip
Make a large batch of these and freeze in 2-cup portions in freezer-safe resealable bags for up to 1 month. Reheat in a 350°F oven for about 15 minutes, or until warmed through and crispy.

Baked Samosa Cups Continued

6   Center 1 tortilla in each muffin well, pushing it in to form a cup. Evenly divide the filling among the tortillas.

7   Bake for 10 to 12 minutes, or until the tortillas are crispy and golden brown and the filling is bubbling.

8   Remove and let rest for at least 2 minutes before serving.

Quinoa Moussaka

Serves 4 to 6

Moussaka is most familiar as a Greek eggplant casserole, though cuisines all over the Middle East and along the Aegean Sea have their own version. Typically, it is baked with ground meat in a white sauce made from flour and butter. Here, we're using quinoa instead of beef and adding a light, creamy topping after cooking for a healthier vegetarian twist. It's almost like eggplant lasagna!

2 large eggplants, peeled and thinly sliced lengthwise

Kosher salt

Freshly ground black pepper

4 tablespoons extra-virgin olive oil, divided

2 garlic cloves, minced

2 teaspoons ground coriander

1½ teaspoons dried oregano

1 teaspoon ground cumin

½ teaspoon ground cinnamon

1 (28-ounce) can organic crushed tomatoes with their juice

1 cup dried quinoa, rinsed well and drained

⅓ cup golden raisins

Nonstick cooking spray

½ cup plain low-fat Greek yogurt

1. Season the eggplant with salt and pepper. Let sit for 5 minutes. Using a paper towel, blot any excess moisture from the eggplant.
2. Heat 2 tablespoons of olive oil in a large sauté pan or skillet over medium-high heat, until it shimmers.
3. Working with 4 slices at a time, add the eggplant to the pan and sauté on each side for about 5 minutes, until golden brown. The whole process should take about 20 minutes. Transfer the cooked slices to paper towels to drain.
4. Heat the remaining 2 tablespoons of olive oil in the same pan over medium-high heat.

Continued ▸

Quinoa Moussaka Continued

5   Add the garlic, coriander, oregano, cumin, and cinnamon, and season with salt and pepper. Cook for 1 to 2 minutes, or until fragrant.

6   Stir in the tomatoes, quinoa, and raisins. Reduce the heat to low and simmer for 15 minutes, or until the tomatoes begin to break down and the quinoa and raisins have plumped. Taste and season with salt and pepper, as needed.

7   Preheat the broiler and position a rack in the top third of the oven. Coat an 8-by-11-inch baking dish with cooking spray.

8   Lay down half the eggplant slices in the bottom of the prepared baking dish. Pour most of the tomato-quinoa mixture over the top. Lay down the remaining eggplant slices and top with the final bit of sauce.

9   Broil for 6 to 8 minutes, or until slightly crusty and bubbly. Remove from the oven and let sit for at least 5 minutes before serving with a dollop of yogurt.

Chicken and Artichoke Cannelloni
with Pesto Cream

Serves 4

Hand-rolled cannelloni with leftover chicken, artichokes, and cheese makes an easy and elegant entertaining dish. Use lasagna sheets instead of precooked cannelloni tubes to save yourself the trouble of trying to fill cooked, hollow pasta.

Nonstick cooking spray

2 tablespoons plus 1 teaspoon kosher salt, divided, plus more as needed

1 (14-ounce) can quartered artichoke hearts, drained and rinsed

1 cup shredded mozzarella cheese, plus more for topping

Grated zest of 2 lemons, divided

1¾ cups fresh basil, chopped, divided

1¼ cup grated Parmesan cheese, divided

1½ teaspoons freshly ground black pepper, plus more as needed

1 shredded cooked chicken breast such as Lemon, Rosemary, and Garlic (page 72)

10 whole-grain lasagna sheets

3 garlic cloves, minced

⅓ cup pine nuts, toasted

¾ cup extra-virgin olive oil

1 cup half-and-half

1. Preheat oven to 375°F. Coat a 9-by-13-inch baking dish with cooking spray and set aside. Fill a large bowl with ice water and set aside.

2. In a large pot, combine the water and 2 tablespoons of salt. Place the pot over high heat and bring to a boil.

Continued ▸

Active time:
50 minutes

Total time:
1 hour, 15 minutes

Serving tip
Serve with a lovely Italian ciabatta or focaccia bread to soak up all that delicious pesto cream!

Chicken and Artichoke Cannelloni with Pesto Cream Continued

3   In a food processor, combine the artichoke hearts, mozzarella cheese, zest of 1 lemon, ¼ cup of basil, and ¼ cup of Parmesan cheese, and season with salt and pepper. Process for 1 minute, until the ingredients are smooth and combined but not fully puréed. Scoop the artichoke filling into a bowl and fold in the chicken. Refrigerate for at least 10 minutes before using.

4   Add the lasagna sheets to the boiling water. Cook for 7 to 8 minutes, or until pliable. Drain the pasta into a colander. Place the lasagna noodles in the bowl of ice water.

5   While the lasagna cooks, in the same food processor bowl (no need to clean it), combine the garlic, remaining lemon zest, remaining 1½ cups of basil, remaining 1 cup of Parmesan cheese, pine nuts, 1½ teaspoons of salt, and 1½ teaspoons of pepper. Process for 1 minute to chop everything. With the processor running, add the olive oil in a thin, steady stream until combined.

6   Lay the lasagna sheets on a work surface. Place 3 heaping tablespoons of artichoke filling in the lower third of a lasagna sheet. Roll the sheet around the filling and place it into the prepared baking dish. Repeat with the remaining filling and noodles. Top the cannelloni with the pesto and sprinkle with Parmesan cheese. Pour the half-and-half into the bottom of the baking dish. Cover the baking dish with foil.

7   Bake for 15 to 20 minutes, or until warmed through and bubbling. Let rest for at least 2 minutes before removing foil and serving.

French Onion Quiche

Serves 6

This quiche has all the delicious flavors of a French onion soup. Caramelized onions and nutty Gruyère cheese deliver a quiche sure to please with its simple ingredients and developed rich flavors. Serve warm, cold, or at room temperature for breakfast, lunch, or dinner.

Nut-Free
Vegetarian

Active time:
40 minutes

Total time:
1 hour

Cooking tip
The key to blind baking—baking the unfilled pie crust to preserve its shape—and to caramelizing the onions is to leave them alone as they cook. Resist the urge to jostle either to get the best results.

Nonstick cooking spray

1 frozen pie crust, thawed, unrolled

2 cups dried beans, for baking the crust

2 tablespoons unsalted butter

5 onions, thinly sliced

Kosher salt

Freshly ground black pepper

½ cup heavy (whipping) cream

5 large eggs, beaten

2 cups reduced-fat milk

⅓ cup shredded Gruyère cheese

2 tablespoons fresh thyme leaves, chopped

1 Preheat the oven to 350°F and position a rack in the center of the oven. Coat a 9-inch pie plate with cooking spray.

2 Fit the pie crust into the prepared pie plate. Using your thumb and index finger, crimp the edges of the crust into pointy ridges, or trim the excess flat against the plate. Poke holes in the crust all over with a fork. Place a round cake pan inside the crust and fill it with the dried beans to weigh it down.

3 Bake for 10 to 15 minutes, or until the crust is golden brown and crispy around the edges. Remove from the oven, remove the pan with the beans from the crust (once cooled, you can save the beans to reuse for your next pie crust), and bake the crust for 5 minutes more to crisp the bottom. Remove the crust from the oven and set aside to cool for at least 10 minutes.

Continued ▶

French Onion Quiche Continued

4   Meanwhile, in a medium sauté pan or skillet over medium heat, melt the butter.

5   Add the onions and season with salt and pepper. Sauté the onions for at least 20 minutes, until they are amber brown and caramelized.

6   Add the cream to deglaze the pan, stirring with a wooden spoon to loosen any browned bits stuck to the bottom. Remove the pan from the heat and set aside.

7   In a medium bowl, whisk the eggs, milk, Gruyère cheese, and thyme, and season with salt and pepper. Set aside.

8   Add the onions to the pie crust, spreading them in an even layer. Pour the egg mixture over the onions. Place the filled pie plate on a sheet pan for extra support and place it in the oven.

9   Bake for 20 to 25 minutes, or until the filling is set but jiggles just slightly when moved. Remove from the oven and let cool for 5 minutes before serving.

Apple-Pecan Stuffed Turkey Breast

Serves 4

An autumnal dish at its finest, this turkey breast might seem complicated, but is really quite simple. Extra care for technique ensures this
poultry and its pan gravy turn out flavorful and delicious. Plus, this
turkey breast cooks in a fraction of the time a whole bird takes, so it's
great for Thanksgiving (or Friendsgiving) in a pinch.

3 tablespoons unsalted butter, divided

½ onion, cut into small dice

1 Honeycrisp apple, peeled, cored, and cut into small dice

¼ cup pecans, chopped

¼ cup dried cranberries

Kosher salt

Freshly ground black pepper

1 cup apple cider, divided

2 tablespoons chopped fresh sage

1 (2-to-3 pound) boneless turkey breast, at room temperature

½ cup low-sodium chicken broth

1½ teaspoons apple cider vinegar

1   Preheat the oven to 400°F. Place a wire rack inside a roasting pan.

2   In a medium sauté pan or skillet over medium heat, melt 2 table-
    spoons of butter. Add the onion and sauté for about 3 minutes
    until translucent. Add the apple, pecans, and cranberries. Gener-
    ously season with salt and pepper. Sauté for 5 minutes until the
    filling is soft.

3   Add ½ cup of apple cider to deglaze the pan, stirring with a
    wooden spoon to loosen any browned bits stuck to the bottom.
    Sprinkle the sage over the filling and toss to combine. Pour into a
    bowl and let cool.

Continued ▶

Gluten-Free

Grain-Free

Active time:
1 hour

Total time:
1 hour, 30 minutes

Cooking tip
The technique of cutting
the turkey breast in half
as we do here is known as
butterflying.

Cooking tip
In this case, the "thickest
part of the breast" could
be at the top of the
breast, like a chicken
breast, or where the two
pieces of turkey overlap
to enclose the filling.
Check both to ensure
your meat is cooked
thoroughly.

4 Make an incision into the center of the turkey breast from the side without cutting all the way through the breast. Open the turkey breast like a book and sandwich between two sheets of plastic wrap. Pound it out slightly with a rolling pin, until about ¾-inch thick all around. Season the inside surface of the meat with salt and pepper.

5 Place the filling in the center of the turkey breast, leaving an unfilled edge all the way around. Fold over the turkey breast to close it over the filling and use toothpicks to hold the breast closed and secure the filling inside. Season with salt and pepper. Place the stuffed turkey on the rack in the roasting pan.

6 Pour the chicken broth and remaining ½ cup of apple cider into the pan.

7 Roast for 25 to 30 minutes total (11 minutes per pound), basting frequently with the pan juices, or until the internal temperature of the thickest part of the turkey breast registers 165°F measured on an instant-read thermometer (see tip).

8 Remove the turkey from the oven, tent it with aluminum foil, and let rest for 10 minutes. Transfer the turkey to a cutting board.

9 Pour the pan juices into a small saucepan and place the pan over medium heat. Cook for 7 to 8 minutes to reduce.

10 Add the vinegar and remaining tablespoon of butter to the pan juices to make gravy. Remove the toothpicks, slice the turkey breast, and serve with the gravy.

Shallot, Garlic, and Herb Chicken Thighs

Serves 2

Dressed in classic and simple flavors, this chicken never fails to impress. Plus, it pairs with almost anything at any time of the year!

4 chicken thighs, at room temperature

Kosher salt

Freshly ground black pepper

3 tablespoons cold unsalted butter, divided

2 tablespoons extra-virgin olive oil, divided

2 medium shallots, thinly sliced

3 garlic cloves, thinly sliced

6 tablespoons white grape juice

2 tablespoons freshly squeezed lemon juice, plus more as needed

¾ cup low-sodium chicken broth

6 thyme sprigs, leaves removed and chopped

2 tablespoons fresh tarragon leaves, thinly sliced (chiffonade)

1 Preheat the oven to 400°F.

2 Generously season the chicken with salt and pepper. Set aside for 5 minutes.

3 In an ovenproof skillet or Dutch oven over medium-high heat, melt 1 tablespoon of butter with 1 tablespoon of olive oil.

4 Arrange the chicken in a single layer on the bottom of the pan. Sear for 7 to 8 minutes, or until the skin is golden brown and crispy. Remove from pan and set aside. Drain any excess fat from the pan.

5 Return the skillet to medium heat and add the remaining tablespoon of olive oil, shallots, and garlic. Sauté for about 5 minutes, or until the shallots and garlic are fragrant and light golden brown.

Continued ▶

Gluten-Free

Grain-Free

Nut-Free

🕐

Active time:
35 minutes

Total time:
45 minutes

Ingredient tip
If you prefer to use boneless, skinless chicken breasts, season the breasts as you would the thighs and skip directly to sautéing the shallots and garlic (step 5). Add the chicken breasts to the pan, and proceed as indicated, testing the temperature at the thickest part of the breast at 15 to 18 minutes instead of 20.

Shallot, Garlic, and Herb Chicken Thighs   Continued

6   Remove the skillet from the heat and add the grape juice, lemon juice, and chicken broth to deglaze the pan, stirring with a wooden spoon to loosen any browned bits stuck to the bottom. Return the chicken to the pan in a single layer. Add the thyme.

7   Bake, uncovered, for 20 minutes, or until the chicken juices run entirely clear at the thickest part of the thigh away from the bone. Remove from the pan and let rest.

8   Meanwhile, whisk the pan juices to distribute the liquid evenly. Place the pan over medium-low heat and swirl in the remaining 2 tablespoons of butter. Taste and season with salt, pepper, and lemon juice, as needed.

9   Ladle the sauce onto a serving platter. Place the chicken thighs, skin-side up, on top of the sauce. Sprinkle with tarragon and serve immediately so that the skin stays crispy!

Steak Tacos
with Refried Black Beans

Serves 4

Brightly flavored chimichurri sauce tenderizes and tops flavorful skirt steak in these Argentinian-inspired tacos. Refried black beans make a warm, quick, and creamy canvas for the steak.

⅓ cup red wine vinegar

½ cup fresh parsley, chopped

¼ cup plus 1 tablespoon extra-virgin olive oil, divided

¼ cup fresh oregano leaves, chopped

2¼ teaspoons red pepper flakes, divided, plus more as needed

4 garlic cloves, minced

1 teaspoon kosher salt, plus more as needed

1 teaspoon freshly ground black pepper, plus more as needed

1 pound skirt steak

Nonstick cooking spray

1 (15-ounce) can black beans, drained and rinsed

1 teaspoon ground cumin

10 white corn tortillas, warmed

---

1 In a food processor or a medium bowl, combine the vinegar, parsley, ¼ cup of olive oil, oregano, 1½ teaspoons of red pepper flakes, garlic, salt, and pepper. Pulse for about 1 minute, or stir, to combine the ingredients into a semi-uniform mixture. Pour half the chimichurri into a gallon-size resealable plastic bag and reserve the other half for later.

2 Place the steak into the bag with the chimichurri. Seal and refrigerate for at least 30 minutes or up to 24 hours.

3 Bring the steak to room temperature. Remove it from the bag and discard the excess marinade.

Continued ▶

Dairy-Free

Gluten-Free

Nut-Free

Active time:
20 minutes

Total time:
40 minutes

Cooking tip
What does it mean to slice against the grain? The tissue that makes up meat has fibers that run in one direction. By slicing against the grain, meaning across it, we sever those long strands for a more tender steak. Look for long lines or ridges in your cooked steak and slice perpendicular to them.

Steak Tacos with Refried Black Beans Continued

4   Coat a grill, grill pan, or skillet with cooking spray and preheat it to medium-high heat.

5   Grill the steak for 3 to 4 minutes per side for medium-rare, or until the meat's internal temperature registers 145°F. Cook for 1 to 1½ minutes more for medium and 2 minutes for well done. Let the steak rest for at least 3 minutes before slicing against the grain into thin pieces.

6   Meanwhile, heat the remaining tablespoon of olive oil in a medium sauté pan or skillet over medium heat, until it shimmers.

7   Add the black beans, the remaining ¾ teaspoon of red pepper flakes, and the cumin. Sauté for 5 minutes, or until the beans begin to soften. Taste and season with salt and pepper. Remove the beans from the heat and, using a fork or potato masher, roughly mash the mixture.

8   Spread the refried bean mixture on warmed corn tortillas. Place the sliced steak atop the beans, and drizzle with the reserved chimichurri sauce.

Blueberry, Rosemary, and Balsamic Pork Loin

☑ *Extra Quick* ⋆ *Serves 4*

This tenderloin is a showstopper. Although pork and blueberries sound like an odd combination, the sweetness of the berries melds perfectly with the savory protein. Think Southern barbecue meets five-star restaurant.

1 pork tenderloin, at room temperature

Kosher salt

Freshly ground black pepper

1¼ teaspoons canola oil or grapeseed oil

¼ cup balsamic vinegar

¼ cup water

2 tablespoons honey or agave nectar

1 tablespoon Dijon mustard

2 rosemary sprigs

6 ounces fresh blueberries

1 Preheat the oven to 350°F.

2 Generously season the pork with salt and pepper.

3 Heat the canola oil in an ovenproof skillet over medium-high heat, until it shimmers. Add the pork and sear on all sides to form a brown crust—about 30 seconds per side; 2 to 3 minutes total. Remove the pork from the skillet and set aside.

4 Add the vinegar and water to deglaze the skillet, stirring with a wooden spoon to loosen any browned bits stuck to the bottom.

5 Whisk in the honey and mustard. Add the rosemary sprigs. Nestle the pork onto the rosemary. Spoon some of the sauce over the pork to coat it.

Continued ▶

🔖
Gluten-Free
Grain-Free
Nut-Free

🕐
Active time:
20 minutes

Total time:
30 minutes

Ingredient tip
Use whole-grain Dijon mustard if you can find it. It adds a nice bite and texture to the sauce.

Blueberry, Rosemary, and Balsamic Pork Loin Continued

6 Place the skillet in the oven and roast for 8 to 10 minutes, or until the pork's internal temperature registers 145°F measured on an instant-read thermometer. Remove from the oven, transfer the pork to a clean plate, and tent with aluminum foil. Let rest for 4 minutes before slicing.

7 Place the skillet over high heat and bring the pan juices to a boil. Add the blueberries. Cook for about 6 minutes to reduce the sauce until most of the berries have burst. Remove and discard the rosemary.

8 Drizzle the pork slices with the pan sauce.

Halibut
with Parsley and Pistachios

☑ **Extra Quick** ★ *Serves 4*

A nutty, herbal, and citrusy crust on halibut or whitefish fillets makes for a flavorful entrée that is ready in under a half hour, but tastes like it took much longer.

⅓ cup panko bread crumbs

⅓ cup roasted, salted pistachios, finely chopped

¼ cup fresh parsley, chopped

1 garlic clove, minced

Zest of 1 orange

Kosher salt

Freshly ground black pepper

1½ tablespoons extra-virgin olive oil

4 (6-ounce) halibut fillets, at room temperature, dried, pin bones removed (see tip, page 110)

1 large egg white, beaten with 1 tablespoon water

1   Preheat the oven to 400°F. Line a sheet pan with aluminum foil.

2   In a medium bowl, stir together the panko, pistachios, parsley, garlic, and orange zest, and season with salt and pepper. The overall mixture should look like medium bread crumbs.

3   Stir in the olive oil.

4   Season the halibut fillets with salt and pepper and place them on the prepared sheet pan. Brush the top of each fillet with the egg white wash. Spoon the panko-pistachio mixture on top of the fillets, patting it down slightly to help it adhere to the fish.

5   Bake for 12 to 13 minutes, or until the crust is lightly browned and the internal temperature reaches 145°F on an instant-read thermometer.

6   Remove and let rest for 2 to 3 minutes.

Ingredient tip
If you cannot find halibut, this recipe also works especially well with trout or a whitefish such as cod, pollock, or tilapia. Don't hesitate to buy frozen fish fillets either; good frozen fish often tastes as good or better than "fresh" fish (flash frozen and thawed) at the counter.

Active time:
45 minutes

Total time:
1 hour

Ingredient tip
Look for wheat germ in the cereal aisle. The germ is nutty, hearty, and packed with fiber, making a flavorful binder for this loaf as a replacement for flour or bread crumbs.

Meatless Roast
with Balsamic-Pear Glaze

Serves 6

A homemade walnut-based vegetarian roast makes the perfect centerpiece for a special occasion. A sweet-tart balsamic and pear glaze complements the earthy, nutty flavors perfectly. This recipe requires some extra love and labor, but it's definitely worth it.

- *4 tablespoons unsalted butter, divided*
- *8 ounces white mushrooms, thinly sliced*
- *½ onion, finely diced*
- *2 large eggs, beaten*
- *1¼ tablespoons fresh rosemary leaves, chopped, divided*
- *2 teaspoons ground allspice*
- *1½ teaspoons kosher salt, plus more as needed*
- *1 teaspoon freshly ground black pepper, plus more as needed*
- *1⅔ cups walnuts, chopped and toasted*
- *1 cup wheat germ, plus more for dusting*
- *2 Bosc pears, peeled, cored, and sliced*
- *1 cup water*
- *¼ cup balsamic vinegar*
- *¼ cup blue cheese crumbles (optional)*

1. In a medium sauté pan or skillet over medium heat, melt 2 tablespoons of butter.

2. Add the mushrooms and onion and sauté for 5 to 7 minutes until softened, browned, and onion is translucent. Set aside to cool slightly, about 3 minutes. Transfer to a food processor.

3. Add the beaten eggs, 1½ teaspoons of rosemary, allspice, salt, and pepper. Purée until smooth and thick. Add the walnuts and purée until most of the walnuts are broken up but some texture still remains, about 2 minutes.

4   Add the wheat germ and pulse until the mixture comes together.

5   Dust a work surface with wheat germ and turn the walnut mixture out onto it. Form the mixture into a cylinder and tightly wrap it in plastic wrap, pulling the edges of the plastic taut and rolling until a tight log forms. Twist the ends of the plastic and tuck them under the wrapped roast. Freeze the roast for 10 minutes to firm up.

6   Preheat the oven to 400°F and position a rack in the middle of the oven.

7   In a large ovenproof skillet over medium-high heat, melt the remaining 2 tablespoons of butter.

8   Place the roast in the skillet and sear on all sides, about 2 minutes total, making sure to sear the ends and carefully flipping it as you go. Scatter the pears around the roast and sprinkle the remaining ¾ teaspoon of rosemary over the top. Pour the water and vinegar over the pears and season them with salt and pepper. Cover the skillet with aluminum foil.

9   Bake for 20 to 25 minutes, or until the pears begin to break down and the liquid has reduced substantially.

10 Remove from the oven, remove the foil, and spoon the balsamic sauce all over the top of the roast. Replace the foil and let rest for at least 5 minutes before slicing and serving with the balsamic-pear sauce and blue cheese (if using).

Gluten-Free

Grain-Free

Nut-Free

Active time:

25 minutes

Total time:

30 minutes

Cooking tip

Use a toothpick to secure the prosciutto to the steak so it doesn't unravel when cooking.

Prosciutto-Wrapped Steak

with Mustard Sauce

☑ **Extra Quick** ⋆ **Serves 4**

This is the dinner to cook when you really want to impress. Tender sirloin steak wrapped in lean-but-crispy prosciutto, served with a decadent—but slightly healthier—mustard cream sauce. Save this dish for special occasions because it's the sort of treat that loses its pizzazz if you eat it all the time.

3 tablespoons Dijon mustard, divided

4 (8-ounce) sirloin steaks, at room temperature

8 ounces prosciutto di Parma, sliced

Kosher salt

Freshly ground black pepper

3 tablespoons unsalted butter, divided

2 tablespoons fresh rosemary leaves, chopped

1 shallot, thinly sliced

1 cup low-sodium beef broth

2 tablespoons heavy (whipping) cream

2 tablespoons capers, drained and rinsed

1   Preheat the oven to 400°F and position a rack in the center of the oven.

2   Brush each steak all over with 1 tablespoon of mustard. Wrap 2 slices of prosciutto around each steak. Season with salt and pepper. Set aside.

3   Place an ovenproof skillet over medium-high heat until you can feel the heat radiating off the pan when holding your hand over it (do not touch it!).

4   Add 1 tablespoon of butter to the skillet to melt, swirling it around the pan.

5   Place the steaks in the hot skillet and sear for 1 minute per side (back, front, top, and bottom). Add the remaining 2 tablespoons of butter to melt, spooning it over the steaks to develop a nut-brown, caramelized crust.

6   Place the skillet in the oven and bake the steaks for 6 minutes, flipping them halfway through the baking time to cook evenly for a medium-rare steak. Their internal temperature should register 145°F measured on an instant-read thermometer. Add 2 minutes for medium and 3 minutes for well done.

7   Remove the steaks from the oven and transfer them to a plate. Tent with aluminum foil and let rest for at least 5 minutes.

8   Place the skillet with the pan drippings over medium heat and add the rosemary and shallot. Sauté for about 3 minutes until the shallot is slightly brown and the rosemary is fragrant.

9   Whisk in the remaining 2 tablespoons of mustard.

10 Stir in the beef broth to deglaze the skillet, stirring with a wooden spoon to loosen any browned bits stuck to the bottom. Bring the liquid to a boil. Reduce the heat to a simmer and cook for about 3 minutes.

11 Remove the skillet from the heat and whisk in the cream and capers. Taste the sauce and season with salt and pepper, as needed.

12 Serve the steaks topped with the sauce.

5

SIDES

SNACKS

Nut-Free
Vegetarian

Active time:
10 minutes

Total time:
15 minutes

Cooking tip
To sauté (from the French verb for *to jump*) like the professional chefs, tilt the pan forward slightly, so all the food clusters at the edge (but not so much that it's almost falling out), and then jerk the pan back quickly. The food will roll up and off the lip of the pan and fall near the back of the pan; use a spoon or spatula to stir the ingredients until you master the technique.

Sesame-Soy Green Beans

☑ *Extra Quick ★ Serves 4*

Salty soy and nutty sesame dress up these crisp green beans into a delectable and addictive side or snack. Eat one, and you won't be able to resist another.

2 tablespoons kosher salt	*1 tablespoon toasted sesame oil*
12 ounces green beans, ends trimmed	*2 tablespoons low-sodium soy sauce*
2 tablespoons unsalted butter	*1 tablespoon sesame seeds*

1   Prepare a large bowl of ice water and set aside.

2   Bring a large pot of salted water to a rolling boil. Add the green beans and cook for 3 minutes.

3   Using tongs or a large slotted spoon, transfer the green beans into the bowl of ice water to stop the cooking. Let sit for 2 minutes. The beans should maintain a bright green color. Drain in a colander.

4   In a large nonstick or stainless steel skillet over medium heat, melt the butter. Add the sesame oil. Add the green beans to the skillet and toss to coat. Sauté for 4 minutes, stirring continuously. Stir in the soy sauce and cook for 1 minute more.

5   Sprinkle the green beans with the sesame seeds, toss to distribute evenly, and serve.

Spiced Carrots
with Pistachios

Serves 4

These Middle Eastern–inspired carrots pay homage to the carrot crop's origins in Persia. A spiced honey coating before roasting imbues these carrots with sweetness and a warm heat. Pistachios add a needed crunch.

4 tablespoons butter, melted

2 tablespoons honey

1 teaspoon ground cardamom

1 teaspoon kosher salt

½ teaspoon ground cinnamon

¼ teaspoon ground cloves

¼ teaspoon ground cumin

¼ teaspoon freshly ground black pepper

1 (2-pound) bag baby carrots, at room temperature

½ cup shelled whole pistachios, chopped

1 Preheat the oven to 400°F and position a rack on the lowest level. Line a sheet pan with aluminum foil and set aside.

2 In a large bowl, stir together the melted butter, honey, cardamom, salt, cinnamon, cloves, cumin, and pepper. Add the carrots and toss to coat. Pour the carrots onto the prepared sheet pan in a single layer.

3 Roast on the bottom rack for 15 minutes.

4 Flip the carrots and roast for 10 minutes more, or until fork-tender.

5 Sprinkle the chopped pistachios evenly over the carrots. Roast for a final 5 minutes. Remove from the oven. Scrape the carrots into a bowl and serve immediately.

Gluten-Free
Grain-Free
Vegetarian

Active time:
35 minutes

Total time:
40 minutes

Ingredient tip
If available, use rainbow baby carrots for an explosion of color on the plate! Rainbow baby carrots are becoming more popular and can be found in the produce section of many grocery stores.

Nut-Free
Vegan

Active time:
30 minutes

Total time:
at least 1 hour

Serving tip
Serve these mushrooms as a tasty side to any protein in the book, but they're especially delicious as a comple-ment to Coffee-Rubbed Tofu (page 124).

Balsamic Baked 'Bellos

Serves 6

Sliced portobello mushrooms get an umami marinade of balsamic vinegar, soy sauce, and olive oil, which doubles as the cooking glaze. Simple and scrumptious!

⅓ *cup balsamic vinegar*

¼ *cup low-sodium soy sauce*

⅓ *cup extra-virgin olive oil*

Kosher salt

Freshly ground black pepper

1 pound portobello mushrooms, sliced

1 In medium bowl, whisk the vinegar and soy sauce.
2 While whisking, drizzle in the olive oil and whisk until combined. Season with salt and pepper and whisk to mix.
3 In a gallon-size resealable plastic bag, combine the mushrooms and marinade. Seal the bag and refrigerate for at least 30 minutes or up to 24 hours.
4 Preheat the oven to 375°F.
5 Pour the mushrooms and marinade into an 8-by-11-inch baking dish. Cover the dish with aluminum foil.
6 Bake for 20 to 25 minutes, or until mushrooms are tender. Serve immediately.

Grilled Asparagus
with Citrus-Herb Butter

☑ **Extra Quick** ★ **Serves 4**

Quick-charred asparagus gets a punchy citrus and tarragon topping. This butter works well on most crunchy green vegetables, too!

6 cups water

Kosher salt

2 bunches asparagus, woody ends trimmed

Freshly ground black pepper

4 tablespoons unsalted butter, at room temperature

2 tablespoons grated lemon zest

Juice of ½ lemon

3 tablespoons fresh tarragon leaves, roughly chopped

Nonstick cooking spray

1 Prepare a large bowl of ice water and set aside.

2 Bring a large pot of salted water to a boil.

3 Add the asparagus and cook for 1 to 1½ minutes. Using tongs, transfer the asparagus to the ice water to stop the cooking. Remove the asparagus and dry on paper towels. Generously season the asparagus with salt and pepper.

4 In a medium bowl, stir together the butter, ½ teaspoon of kosher salt, ½ teaspoon of pepper, lemon zest, and lemon juice until combined. Gently fold in the tarragon leaves. Set aside.

5 Coat a grill, grill pan, or skillet with cooking spray and preheat it to medium-high heat.

6 Grill the asparagus for 3 minutes. Flip the asparagus and grill for 3 minutes more. Transfer the asparagus to the bowl with the seasoned butter and toss to coat.

Gluten-Free

Grain-Free

Nut-Free

Vegetarian

🕐

Active time:
20 minutes

Total time:
25 minutes

Variation tip
Use orange or grapefruit zest and juice instead of the lemon to switch it up. Or, if they are in season, use Meyer lemons!

Gluten-Free
Grain-Free
Nut-Free
Vegetarian

Active time:
27 minutes

Total time:
35 minutes

Ingredient tip
If you don't have fresh oregano or do not want to buy it, use 2 tablespoons dried oregano instead.

Lemon and Oregano Potatoes

Serves 4 to 6

This recipe works well with most small potatoes. Roasting the potatoes, but not leaving them uncovered for the full time, ensures they develop some browning but do not fully dry out. Lemon, garlic, and oregano imbue this dish with lots of Mediterranean flavor.

1 pound fingerling potatoes, quartered

4 tablespoons extra-virgin olive oil

Zest of 1 lemon

Juice of 1 lemon

¼ cup fresh oregano leaves, chopped

2 garlic cloves, minced

2 teaspoons kosher salt

½ teaspoon freshly ground black pepper

¼ cup grated Parmesan cheese (optional)

1 Preheat the oven to 400°F and position a rack in the center of the oven.

2 In a 9-by-13-inch baking dish, arrange potatoes in a single layer.

3 In a small bowl, whisk the olive oil, lemon zest, lemon juice, oregano, and garlic until combined. Pour the mixture over the potatoes and stir to coat the potatoes evenly. Season the potatoes with the salt and pepper.

4 Roast for 15 to 20 minutes, or until potatoes start to become fork-tender and are light golden brown around the edges. Tent the pan with aluminum foil and roast for 10 minutes more.

5 Remove from the oven and sprinkle with the Parmesan cheese (if using).

Turnip-Parsnip Mash

☑ Extra Quick ★ Serves 4

If you're craving mashed potatoes but want a healthier option, this is a delicious stand-in that's lower in fat and carbs. The flavors of turnips and parsnips are more delicate than potatoes, and the sour cream, dill, and garlic accentuate them rather than mask them.

1 cup low-sodium vegetable broth

8 ounces turnips, peeled and cut into medium dice

8 ounces parsnips, peeled and cut into medium dice

2 garlic cloves, crushed

½ cup reduced-fat sour cream

¼ cup fresh dill, chopped

1 teaspoon kosher salt, plus more as needed

½ teaspoon freshly ground black pepper, plus more as needed

1 Heat the vegetable broth in a large wide-bottomed pot or Dutch oven over medium heat.

2 Reduce the heat to medium-low. Nestle a metal colander inside the pot without it touching the bottom, or use a steamer basket. Add the turnips, parsnips, and garlic. Cover the pot and steam the vegetables for 20 to 25 minutes, or until parsnips and turnips are fork-tender. Transfer the vegetables and any cooking broth remaining in the pot to a food processor.

3 Add the sour cream, dill, salt, and pepper. Purée until just smooth, or until you reach your desired texture. Taste and season with more salt and pepper, as needed. Pulse to combine.

Gluten-Free

Grain-Free

Nut-Free

Vegetarian

Active time:
25 minutes

Total time:
30 minutes

Serving tip
For some super-comfort family meals, serve this mash alongside Apple-Pecan Stuffed Turkey Breast (page 141), Shallot, Garlic, and Herb Chicken Thighs (page 143), or Blueberry, Rosemary, and Balsamic Pork Loin (page 147) and bask in the praise you'll receive for a restaurant-worthy meal.

Active time:
30 minutes

Total time:
40 minutes

Ingredient tip
Precooked polenta
is often found in the
produce section of your
grocery store, refrigerated
with the tofu and other
vegetarian items. Its
firm texture means these
cakes hold up well to
cooking.

Crispy Polenta Cakes
with Tomato Marmalade

Serves 4

Crisp on the outside, creamy on the inside. These polenta cakes are a crowd pleaser. A jammy, sweet tomato marmalade for topping really makes the flavors sing.

Nonstick cooking spray

⅔ cup panko bread crumbs

2 tablespoons dried basil

Grated zest of ½ lemon

1½ teaspoons kosher salt, divided

1 teaspoon freshly ground black pepper, divided

1 (16- to 18-ounce) tube precooked polenta, cut into ¾-inch-thick rounds

12 ounces cherry tomatoes, quartered

Juice of 1 lemon

¼ cup honey

⅛ teaspoon ground cloves

¼ teaspoon ground nutmeg

1 Preheat the oven to 425°F and position a rack in the middle of the oven. Line a baking sheet with parchment paper and coat the parchment with cooking spray.

2 In a medium bowl, stir together the panko, basil, lemon zest, ½ teaspoon of salt, and ½ teaspoon of pepper.

3 Using a pastry brush or your fingers, moisten a polenta round slightly with some water. Turn it in the bread crumb mixture, coating it completely. Transfer the coated polenta to the prepared baking sheet. Repeat with the remaining polenta rounds.

4 Bake for 15 to 20 minutes, or until golden brown and crispy, flipping the polenta cakes about halfway through the cooking time.

5   Meanwhile, in a small saucepan over high heat, combine the cherry tomatoes, lemon juice, honey, cloves, nutmeg, remaining teaspoon of salt, and remaining ½ teaspoon of pepper. Bring the mixture to a boil. Reduce the heat to low and simmer for 20 to 25 minutes, or until thick, syrupy, and chunky. Stir occasionally to prevent burning, but not too often.

6   Remove the polenta cakes from the oven and let cool for at least 3 minutes. Serve with the tomato marmalade.

Active time:
40 minutes

Total time:
45 minutes

Cooking tip
When two ingredients, such as the basmati and wild rice here, have different cooking times (and different starch to liquid ratios), it's easiest to cook them separately even though it means using another pot. This ensures both ingredients are cooked to the correct doneness. If you start them at the same time in the same pot, one will finish before the other. Learning to time food so that it cooks at the same rate comes with practice.

Wild Rice Pilaf

Serves 6

With two types of rice, nuts, fruit, and spices, this pilaf pairs well with a variety of dishes and makes for a filling side dish. Extra care cooking the rice ensures the grains don't get clumpy (see tip). Use as a side for Apple-Pecan Stuffed Turkey Breast (page 141), Shallot, Garlic, and Herb Chicken Thighs (page 143), Blueberry, Rosemary, and Balsamic Pork Loin (page 147), or something more Middle Eastern or Indian—as pilaf has those same roots—like the Lentil and Chickpea Burgers (page 129).

1¼ cups wild rice, rinsed and drained

6¾ cups low-sodium vegetable broth, divided

3 tablespoons butter, divided

½ cup basmati rice, rinsed and drained

1 leek, halved lengthwise, washed well, and thinly sliced crosswise (light green and white parts)

½ cup sliced almonds

¼ cup dried cranberries

¼ cup golden raisins

1 teaspoon ground turmeric

1 teaspoon kosher salt, plus more as needed

¼ teaspoon freshly ground black pepper, plus more as needed

1   In a medium pot, combine the wild rice, 5 cups of vegetable broth, and 1 tablespoon of butter.

2   In another medium pot, combine the basmati rice, 1½ cups of vegetable broth, and 1 tablespoon of butter.

3   Place each pot over high heat and bring the liquid to a boil. Reduce the heat under each pot to maintain a simmer and cover the pots. Cook the basmati rice for 25 to 30 minutes, or until tender. Set aside the basmati rice.

4   Cook the wild rice for 5 minutes more. Drain.

5   Meanwhile, in a large wide-bottomed sauté pan or skillet over medium heat, melt the remaining tablespoon of butter.

6   Add the leek and sauté for 5 minutes, or until translucent.

7   Add the almonds. Sauté for 3 minutes, or until the almonds are crispy, golden, and fragrant.

8   Add the cranberries, raisins, remaining ¼ cup of vegetable broth, turmeric, salt, and pepper. Adjust the heat to medium-low and simmer for 5 minutes, or until the raisins and cranberries have rehydrated.

9   Fluff the basmati rice with a fork. Add the basmati rice and wild rice to the sauté pan. Stir to combine. Taste and season with more salt and pepper, as needed.

Active time:

15 minutes

Total time:

25 minutes

Variation tip

To give these chips another level of flavor, use browned butter instead of regular butter. In a medium saucepan over medium heat, melt ½ cup (1 stick) of butter. Cook the butter for about 5 minutes, stirring frequently, until the milk solids separate from the fat and caramelize (brown). The butter will smell nutty and look amber. Immediately remove the pan from the heat and stir in an ice cube to stop the cooking.

Lemon and Rosemary Pita Chips

☑ **Extra Quick** ☆ **Makes about 2 cups of pita chips**

There's nothing like warm pita chips to serve with some nice cheese or dips for a quick and easy appetizer when entertaining, or to snack on. These are perfumed with lemon and rosemary—an altogether tantalizing combination.

6 tablespoons unsalted butter

3 tablespoons fresh rosemary leaves, chopped finely

Grated zest of 1 lemon

4 pita breads, halved and sliced into square pieces

1 teaspoon coarse kosher salt

¾ teaspoon cracked black pepper

1 Preheat the oven to 400°F. Line a baking sheet with parchment paper and set aside.

2 In a microwave-safe bowl, melt the butter in the microwave on high power. Then, add the rosemary and lemon zest, and stir to combine.

3 Place the pita pieces on the parchment-lined baking sheet. Pour on the melted butter, and mix around to coat all the pieces. Arrange in a single layer, then season with salt and pepper.

4 Bake for 10 to 12 minutes, or until golden brown, fragrant, and crisp. Cool for at least 5 minutes before serving.

Apple-Cheddar Crisps

☑ *Extra Quick* ★ *Serves 2*

Quick, crunchy, and slightly sweet, these cheese-and-fruit crisps hit the spot. Plus, they're ready in mere minutes. Snack on!

½ cup grated Honeycrisp apple, squeezed of excess water

½ cup Cheddar cheese, grated

½ teaspoon ground cinnamon (optional)

1 Line a large microwave-safe plate with parchment paper.
2 In a small bowl, stir together the grated apple and Cheddar cheese.
3 Place small piles of the apple and Cheddar cheese around the plate. Sprinkle with cinnamon, if using.
4 Microwave on high power for 4 minutes, watching carefully to ensure that the crisps don't burn.
5 Remove from the microwave and let cool for 2 minutes. Remove cooked crisps to a serving dish. Repeat with remaining mixture until you have a plate of crisps.

Gluten-Free
Grain-Free
Nut-Free
Vegetarian

Active time:
5 minutes

Total time:
15 minutes

Variation tip
The apple can also be minced and mixed in, and feel free to substitute whatever grated cheese and fruit or vegetable that you would like. Pear and Fontina, or tomato, Mozzarella, and basil would also be delicious!

Active time:
7 minutes

Total time:
10 minutes

Variation tip
Substitute a non-hydrogenated margarine and agave nectar to make this popcorn vegan!

Honey-Sriracha Popcorn

☑ **Extra Quick** ★ **Serves 4**

Honey and Sriracha lend this popcorn a sweet heat and a nice change of pace from the classic (but often artificial) microwave movie theater–butter snack.

2 tablespoons canola oil or grapeseed oil

⅓ cup popcorn kernels

⅓ to 1 cup peanuts, toasted and chopped (optional)

4 tablespoons unsalted butter

2 tablespoons honey

2 tablespoons Sriracha

¼ teaspoon kosher salt

1 Heat the canola oil in a wide-bottom skillet over medium-high heat, until it shimmers.

2 Add 1 popcorn kernel, cover the skillet, and wait until the kernel pops. Add the rest of the popcorn kernels, cover the skillet, and toss briefly to coat the kernels in the oil. Pop the corn for no more than 4 minutes, or until the popping slows to 1 kernel popping every 5 seconds. Shake the covered pan frequently to prevent the popcorn from burning. Remove the popcorn from the heat and pour it into a large bowl. Add in the peanuts (if using).

3 Turn off the heat. In the hot skillet, melt the butter.

4 Stir in the honey and Sriracha to blend. Pour the mixture over the hot popcorn.

5 Pour everything back into the skillet, cover it, and toss well to coat the popcorn evenly in the butter. Return everything to the bowl.

6 Sprinkle the popcorn with salt.

N[o]tella

☑ Extra Quick ⋆ **Makes 1½ cups**

For many, Nutella is a guilty pleasure. This version is homemade to avoid the hidden sugars and preservatives, but that doesn't make it any less delicious! Spread it on toast or pancakes, drizzle it over ice cream, or make N[o]tella Lava Cakes with Strawberries (page 190).

1 cup hazelnuts

8 ounces bittersweet chocolate, chopped

¼ cup vegetable oil

1½ tablespoons honey

¼ cup milk

½ teaspoon vanilla extract

¼ teaspoon kosher salt

1. Preheat the oven to 350°F and position a rack in the center.
2. Spread the hazelnuts in a single layer on a sheet pan.
3. Roast for 10 to 12 minutes until golden and fragrant.
4. Remove the nuts from the oven and let cool for 3 minutes. Place the hazelnuts in a clean kitchen towel and rub them together to remove as much of their skins as possible (see tip, page 26). Transfer the nuts to a cutting board and roughly chop them. Set aside.
5. In a medium microwave-safe bowl, combine the chocolate, vegetable oil, and honey. Microwave on high for 30 seconds. Stir the mixture. Continue to microwave in 30-second intervals, stirring after each, until the mixture is liquid and combined.
6. In a processor, process the hazelnuts for 2 minutes, or until the mixture is a thick paste.

Continued ▶

Gluten-Free
Grain-Free
Vegetarian

Active time:
20 minutes

Total time:
25 minutes

Ingredient tip
This will keep, refrigerated in an airtight container, for up to 2 weeks.

N[o]tella Continued

7　With the processor running, slowly drizzle in the chocolate mixture. Process for 2 minutes more.

8　With the machine off, add the milk, vanilla extract, and salt. Pulse to combine. Spoon into a sealable jar, or enjoy immediately.

Orange, Honey, and Vanilla Yogurt Dip

Makes about 1⅓ cups

Orange, honey, and vanilla combine in this sweet, floral, creamy dip that is perfect for fresh fruit, in parfaits, or for topping breakfast foods.

1 cup plain nonfat Greek yogurt

¼ cup reduced-fat sour cream

1 tablespoon vanilla bean paste, or the seeds of 1 vanilla bean removed from a split (lengthwise) and scraped bean

2 tablespoons honey

Zest of 1 orange

1 tablespoon freshly squeezed orange juice

¼ teaspoon kosher salt

In a medium bowl, stir together the yogurt, sour cream, vanilla paste, honey, orange zest, orange juice, and salt. Cover the bowl and refrigerate for at least 30 minutes before serving.

Gluten-Free
Grain-Free
Nut-Free
Vegetarian

Active time:
5 minutes

Total time:
40 minutes

Ingredient tip
No vanilla bean paste or beans? No worries. Although the flavor won't be quite as rich nor the dip as pleasing to the eye, you can substitute 1 tablespoon vanilla extract.

Active time:
30 minutes

Total time:
35 minutes

Cooking tip
If you don't have a food processor, mince the roasted garlic. In a medium bowl, combine the garlic, chickpeas, tahini, lemon juice, cumin, coriander, salt, and pepper. Using a potato masher, mash the ingredients until smooth. Stir in the olive oil and finish as directed.

Roasted Garlic Hummus

Makes about 1¼ cups

Ah, hummus—the ubiquitous entertainment go-to and protein-packed afternoon snack. This version makes it just a bit more interesting with roasted garlic.

4 garlic cloves, peeled

1 (15-ounce) can all-natural chickpeas, drained and rinsed

2 tablespoons tahini

Juice of 1 lemon

1½ teaspoons ground cumin

1½ teaspoons ground coriander

1½ teaspoons kosher salt

½ teaspoon freshly ground black pepper

5 tablespoons extra-virgin olive oil, plus more for serving

¼ teaspoon paprika

1 Preheat oven to 400°F and position a rack in the middle of the oven.

2 Place the garlic cloves on a small sheet pan. Roast for 20 to 25 minutes, or until golden brown and aromatic. Remove from the oven and let cool.

3 In a food processor, combine the roasted garlic, chickpeas, tahini, lemon juice, cumin, coriander, salt, and pepper. Process until puréed.

4 With the processor running, drizzle in the olive oil. Spoon the hummus into a serving bowl.

5 Drizzle with more olive oil (if desired), and sprinkle with paprika.

Grilled Pineapple-Serrano Guacamole

☑ *Extra Quick* ★ *Makes about 5 cups*

Sweet, caramelized grilled pineapple, spicy serrano chili, citrus, and cilantro make this guacamole a delight. Serve with multigrain or corn tortilla chips.

Nonstick cooking spray

½ peeled, cored fresh pineapple, thickly sliced

1 serrano chili, halved and seeded

4 avocados, halved, pitted (see tip, page 19), and diced

1 small red onion, cut into small dice

Juice of 1½ limes

¼ cup fresh cilantro, chopped

1 garlic clove, minced

½ teaspoon ground cumin

1 teaspoon kosher salt, plus more as needed

½ teaspoon freshly ground black pepper, plus more as needed

1 Coat a grill, grill pan, or skillet with cooking spray and preheat it to medium-high heat.

2 Place the pineapple slices and serrano chili halves on the grill. Cook for 3 minutes. Flip chilies and cook for 3 minutes more. Remove chilies from the grill and set aside to cool for 5 minutes. Cut the pineapple and the chili into a fine dice.

3 In a medium bowl, combine the avocado, red onion, lime juice, cilantro, garlic, cumin, salt, pepper, and diced chili. Using a fork, mash the ingredients into a chunky paste.

4 Fold in the pineapple.

Active time:
20 minutes

Total time:
30 minutes

◇

Ingredient tip
Avocados tend to turn an ugly brown color quickly when exposed to air. In this recipe, the acid from the lime juice and the pineapple help it retain its original color for about 2 days. Store any leftover guacamole in an airtight container with a piece of plastic wrap touching its surface to reduce contact with air.

7

DRINKS and DESSERTS

Gluten-Free

Grain-Free

Nut-Free

Vegan

Active time:

10 minutes

Total time:

40 minutes

Cooking tip

It is much easier to juice all the citrus if you roll the fruit on the counter before slicing it in half and use a citrus reamer, either over a bowl or one with a tray. The former technique loosens the fruit membranes for maximum juiciness; the latter is far more efficient than just a fork and is worth the extra investment. If you don't have a reamer, use a fork.

Tangerine, Lime, and Mint Spritzer

Serves 4 to 5

This light and refreshing citrus and sparkling water spritzer is a lovely drink to sip on a hot day.

¼ cup fresh mint, chopped

2 tablespoons agave nectar

1 liter sparkling water

3 cups freshly squeezed tangerine juice, from room-temperature tangerines

1 cup freshly squeezed lime juice, from room-temperature limes

1 cup ice cubes

1　In a small bowl, using a wooden spoon, muddle the mint (crush the leaves to release the oils) with the agave.

2　In a pitcher, stir together the sparkling water, muddled agave and mint, tangerine juice, and lime juice. Chill for at least 30 minutes before serving.

3　Using a fine-mesh strainer set over a bowl, strain out the mint leaves. Return the spritzer to the pitcher, add the ice, and serve.

Hibiscus Ginger Tea

Serves 4 to 6

Hibiscus petals, ginger, and orange zest make a slightly sweet and sharp herbal tea that can be served warm or cold.

2 large pieces orange zest

1 (1-inch) piece fresh ginger, peeled and cut into 1-inch rounds

12 cups water, divided

¼ cup agave nectar, or honey

4 organic hibiscus flower tea bags

Juice of ½ orange

2 cups ice cubes (optional)

1. In a pitcher, combine the orange zest and ginger. Set aside.
2. In a small pan over high heat, bring 8 cups of water and the agave to a boil. Remove the pot from the heat, add the tea bags, and let the tea steep for 4 minutes.
3. Pour the hot tea over the orange zest and ginger in the pitcher and let steep for 10 minutes. Remove and discard the tea bags. Using a slotted spoon, remove and discard the orange zest and ginger.
4. Stir in the orange juice.
5. If serving warm, pour the tea into mugs.
6. If serving cold, add the remaining 4 cups of water to the pitcher along with the ice (if using). Chill for at least 30 minutes before serving over ice.

Gluten-Free
Grain-Free
Nut-Free

Active time:
15 minutes

Total time:
45 minutes

Cooking tip
How do you get orange zest without a zester? Using a paring knife, cut off a thin section of orange peel. If there's any white, spongy material on the back (the bitter pith), carefully remove as much of it as possible with your knife. Don't press down too much while removing this pith or you'll lose all that lovely orange oil.

Gluten-Free

Grain-Free

Nut-Free

Vegan

Active time:

5 minutes

Total time:

2 hours

Serving tip

If you want to make your drinks look more impressive, chill your glasses slightly in the refrigerator or freezer. Rub the rims with a lime wedge and dip them into sugar before pouring in the blitz.

Strawberry, Watermelon, and Basil Blitz

Serves 4

This refreshing ice-cold, strawberry watermelon mocktail makes the perfect drink to transform an ordinary summer day into instant vacation mode. Basil adds an interesting herbal note.

6 ounces strawberries

½ seedless watermelon, cut into large dice

16 ounces coconut water, chilled

2 tablespoons fresh basil leaves, chopped

Juice of ½ lime

1 Put strawberries and watermelon cubes on a sheet pan lined with parchment paper and place in the freezer. Freeze for about 2 hours, or until frozen solid.

2 In a blender, combine the strawberries, watermelon, coconut water, basil, and lime juice. Blend for 2 minutes, or until smooth. Pour into glasses to serve.

Mango-Raspberry Lassi

☑ *Extra Quick* ☆ *Serves 4*

A pink-tinged Indian-spiced yogurt smoothie with the distinct flavors of ginger and cardamom delivers a delicious, creamy, protein-packed beverage. Plus, the turmeric adds some anti-inflammatory agents without altering the flavor too much.

6 ounces frozen raspberries	*3 tablespoons honey or agave nectar*
1 cup diced frozen mango	*½ teaspoon ground ginger*
½ cup plain Greek yogurt	*½ teaspoon ground turmeric*
½ cup cold water	*½ teaspoon ground cardamom*

In a blender, combine the raspberries, mango, yogurt, water, honey, ginger, turmeric, and cardamom. Blend for 2 minutes, or until smooth. Pour into glasses to serve.

Gluten-Free
Grain-Free
Nut-Free
Vegetarian

Active time:
5 minutes

Total time:
15 minutes

Ingredient tip

It's perfectly fine to use pre-frozen fruit for these smoothies, but you can also freeze fresh fruit. Here's how: After washing and drying your fruit, spread it out in a single layer on a sheet pan or plate and freeze until solid. Then place the frozen fruit into an airtight freezer bag until you're ready to use it.

Dairy-Free
Gluten-Free
Grain-Free
Vegetarian

Active time:
5 minutes

Total time:
2 hours

Ingredient tip
It's easier to slice bananas before freezing them rather than after. Spread out the banana coins in a single layer on a sheet pan or plate and freeze until solid.

Banana Mocha Shake

Serves 4

Nicknamed the "energizer monkey" shake, this banana mocha frappe will charge you up any time of the day. Also, it comes together in a flash.

2 bananas, sliced

½ cup almond or coconut milk

¼ cup ice cubes

2 tablespoons instant espresso powder

2 tablespoons unsweetened cocoa powder

1 tablespoon honey or agave nectar

1 Put banana slices on a sheet pan lined with parchment paper and place in the freezer. Freeze for about 2 hours, or until frozen solid.

2 In a blender, combine the bananas, milk, ice cubes, espresso powder, cocoa powder, and honey. Blend for 2 minutes, or until smooth. Pour into glasses to serve.

Affogato Mexicano

☑ Extra Quick ★ **Serves 2**

Doubling as both drink and dessert, this sweet treat fuses Italian technique with Mexican spices for an altogether delicious, bittersweet combination. *Affogato* means "drowned" in Italian; here we "drown" some vanilla ice cream in spiced coffee. Note: Do not drink this too late at night, unless you are aiming to stay awake.

1 cup water	⅜ teaspoon ground cinnamon
1⅜ teaspoons instant espresso powder	⅜ teaspoon ground cloves
1 teaspoon unsweetened cocoa powder	⅜ teaspoon cayenne pepper
	4 scoops vanilla ice cream or vanilla coconut ice cream

1. In a small pot over medium heat, bring the water to a simmer.
2. Remove the pot from the heat and add the instant espresso. Let sit for 2 minutes.
3. Whisk in the cocoa powder, cinnamon, cloves, and cayenne pepper. Let sit for 2 minutes more to infuse.
4. Place two scoops of ice cream in each glass. Pour the hot coffee mixture over the ice cream until it is almost covered. Serve immediately with a tall spoon.

Gluten-Free
Grain-Free
Vegetarian

Active time:
15 minutes

Total time:
20 minutes

Cooking tip
Top with chocolate shavings for extra taste and texture.

Active time:
10 minutes

Total time:
25 minutes

Ingredient tip
For best results, use a homogenized peanut butter, not a natural variety where the oil must be continuously reincorporated.

5-Ingredient Peanut Butter Pretzel Snaps

☑ **Extra Quick** ⋆ **Makes 12 cookies**

Slightly sweet, nutty, and salty, these simple cookies are irresistible. When you crave them, you can whip them up in under 30 minutes with pantry staples. In other words, they're ready in a snap!

1 cup creamy peanut butter

1 cup lightly packed dark brown sugar

1 large egg

1 teaspoon vanilla extract

¼ cup pretzels, crushed, plus 12 whole twists for topping

Nonstick cooking spray

1 Preheat the oven to 350°F. Line a sheet pan with parchment paper and set aside.

2 In a medium bowl, stir together the peanut butter, brown sugar, egg, and vanilla extract until well combined.

3 Fold in the crushed pretzels.

4 Coat a ¼-cup measuring cup with cooking spray and use it to scoop the dough into 12 cookies, placing them about 2 inches apart on the prepared sheet pan. Flatten each cookie slightly, then press a pretzel into the top of each cookie.

5 Bake for 10 minutes, or until slightly golden around the edges. The cookies will be very soft at first. Cool for at least 5 minutes on the sheet pan before attempting to transfer to a cooling rack to finish cooling.

Cherry Chocolate Sherbet

Serves 6

This creamy, semi-frozen treat is made in the food processor. You can serve it right after mixing, though a quick chill does it good. Cherry, chocolate, and almond make an altogether decadent, though simple, dessert.

3 cups frozen pitted dark cherries	*¼ teaspoon kosher salt*
4 ounces sweetened condensed milk	*2 ounces dark chocolate, shaved*
¼ teaspoon almond extract	*2 ounces sliced almonds, toasted*

1 In a food processor, combine the cherries, condensed milk, almond extract, and salt. Purée for about 2 minutes, or until smooth and thick.
2 Either scoop and serve (like soft-serve) once blended, or pour the mixture into a small baking dish, cover it with plastic wrap, and chill for 45 minutes before serving.
3 Top with shaved chocolate and toasted almonds.

Gluten-Free
Grain-Free
Vegetarian

Active time:
5 minutes

Total time:
50 minutes, if chilled

Variation tip
Use different fruits, such as raspberries or strawberries instead of cherries if you don't like them. Once you've mastered this recipe, develop your own flavor combinations (for instance, raspberry, pistachio, and white chocolate—yum!).

Nut-Free
Vegetarian

Active time:
30 minutes

Total time:
35 minutes

Ingredient tip

To segment oranges, after peeling, hold the fruit in your hand over a small bowl. Using a paring knife, cut down into the fruit closely along the membranes (the small white lines) on each side of a segment to release it, letting it fall into the bowl (which will also capture the juices). As you work your way around the orange, hold back the empty membranes with your thumb. When finished, squeeze the membranes to release their remaining juice into the bowl.

Blood Orange and Vanilla Crêpes

Serves 6

A crêpe is a very thin pancake that can be either sweet or savory. These orange-sauced crêpes, stuffed with a creamy vanilla mascarpone cheese, make a light, simple, satisfying dessert.

6 ounces mascarpone cheese, at room temperature

1 tablespoon vanilla extract

Grated zest of 1 blood orange

1 cup milk

2 large eggs

½ cup all-purpose flour

4 tablespoons sugar, divided

½ teaspoon kosher salt

Nonstick cooking spray

2 blood oranges, peeled, segmented, and membranes juiced

1 teaspoon ground cinnamon

½ teaspoon ground cloves

1 In a small bowl, stir together the mascarpone cheese, vanilla, and orange zest. Set aside.

2 In a medium bowl, combine the milk, eggs, flour, 2 tablespoons of sugar, and the salt. Whisk until smooth and combined, no more, no less—you do not want to overmix the batter.

3 Place an 8-inch nonstick skillet over medium heat and generously coat it with cooking spray.

4 Add ¼ cup of batter to the skillet. It should sizzle just slightly. Pick up the skillet and roll the batter around in a circle until no liquid remains. Cook for 2 minutes, or until you can see the bottom of the crêpe lift up from the pan. Using a rubber spatula, gently release the edges of the crepe and tip the crêpe onto a plate. Repeat with the remaining batter, generously coating the pan with cooking spray before cooking each new crêpe.

5   Return the skillet to medium heat and add the remaining 2 tablespoons of sugar to melt and slightly caramelize (turn golden brown).

6   Add the blood orange segments and juice, cinnamon, and cloves and toss to combine. If the sauce is too thick, stir in a bit of water, 1 tablespoon at a time. Simmer for 3 minutes.

7   Place the crêpes on a work surface and evenly divide the mascarpone mixture among them, making a line down the center of the crêpe. Fold each crêpe in half, then in half again.

8   Place 2 crêpes on each plate. Evenly spoon the warm sauce over each to coat, dividing the orange segments among them. Serve immediately.

Active time:
25 minutes

Total time:
45 minutes

Ingredient tip
Canned "cream of coconut" is often found with the Latin foods in most grocery stores. If you cannot find it or want more control over the sugar in this dessert, use plain "coconut cream" (an unsweetened, not-condensed version usually found with the Thai foods), or the solids from an unshaken can of full-fat coconut milk, and add sugar (or your choice of natural sweetener) to taste.

No-Bake Coconut Cheesecakes
with Passion Fruit Sauce

Serves 12

Bright passion fruit–lime sauce and creamy coconut cheesecakes tempt in this tropical-themed dessert. Fresh passion fruit is on sale from late spring through early winter but can be difficult to find fresh. Frozen passion fruit is usually available with the frozen fruits in your grocery store. If you can find them fresh, choose ones with wrinkled, deep purple skins.

1¼ cups all-natural gingersnap cookie crumbs

4 tablespoons unsalted butter, melted

1 (15-ounce) can cream of coconut, drained

8 ounces reduced-fat cream cheese, at room temperature

Juice of 1 lime, or 2 limes if using mango nectar, divided

2 teaspoons vanilla extract, divided

¼ teaspoon kosher salt

¾ cup unsweetened shredded coconut

1 cup passion fruit pulp, fresh or frozen, or mango nectar

1 tablespoon cornstarch

1 Line each well in a standard muffin tin with plastic wrap, extending slightly over the top of each well.

2 In a medium bowl, stir together the cookie crumbs and melted butter until combined. Evenly divide the crust mixture among the prepared wells and press them down with the back of a spoon or your fingers to make a crust about ½-inch thick. Chill for 15 minutes to solidify the crusts.

3　Meanwhile, place the cream of coconut in a small bowl and, using a whisk or handheld electric mixer, beat it until soft peaks form, about 4 minutes. Set aside.

4　In a medium bowl, combine the cream cheese, half of the lime juice, 1 teaspoon of vanilla extract, and the salt. Using a clean whisk or beaters, beat for 2 to 3 minutes, until light and fluffy.

5　Using a spatula, gently fold the whipped coconut cream and ¼ cup of coconut into the cream cheese mixture. Spoon the filling into the crusts until the cheesecake mixture peaks just over the top. Freeze for 20 minutes.

6　In a small saucepan over medium-low heat, warm the passion fruit pulp.

7　In a small bowl, stir together the remaining half of the lime juice and cornstarch until the cornstarch dissolves. Pour the cornstarch mixture into the passion fruit pulp and bring the mixture to a simmer. Cook for 5 minutes until warmed and slightly thickened. Remove from the heat and stir in the remaining teaspoon of vanilla.

8　In a small dry skillet over medium heat, toast the remaining ½ cup of coconut for about 5 minutes, or until light golden brown.

9　Using the plastic wrap, carefully remove the cheesecakes from the muffin tin.

10　Serve each mini cheesecake with a spoonful of the warm passion fruit sauce on the side and sprinkled with toasted coconut.

Nut Free
Vegetarian

Active time:
45 minutes

Total time:
55 minutes

Cooking tip
Toasting nuts or seeds is easy. Place them in a small dry skillet over medium heat and cook for about 5 minutes, stirring frequently and watching closely, until the nuts or seeds brown slightly and begin to smell fragrant and, often, nutty.

Black Sesame and Banana Napoleons

Serves 6

Napoleons are stacks of pastry, filling, and cream. This quick, Asian-inspired version employs baked eggroll wrappers, caramelized bananas, and a nutty, slightly sweet black sesame cream for an elegant dessert for a special occasion.

2 tablespoons sugar

½ teaspoon ground cloves

½ teaspoon ground ginger

6 eggroll wrappers, halved

2 tablespoons melted butter

3 tablespoons black sesame seeds, toasted (see tip)

4 tablespoons honey, divided

1 cup chilled heavy (whipping) cream

4 bananas, sliced on a bias (slant)

Juice of 1 orange

1   Preheat the oven to 350°F and position a rack in the middle of the oven. Line a baking sheet with parchment paper.

2   In a small bowl, stir together the sugar, cloves, and ginger. Set aside.

3   Place the eggroll wrapper halves in a single layer on the prepared baking sheet. Using a pastry brush, brush each with melted butter. Evenly sprinkle the spiced sugar over the wrappers.

4   Bake for 7 to 10 minutes, or until slightly puffed, crispy, and golden brown around the edges. Remove them from the oven and let cool slightly.

5   Place the sesame seeds in a resealable plastic bag. Seal the bag, removing as much air as possible. Using a rolling pin or another heavy object (like a skillet), crush the sesame seeds into a fine powder. Transfer the sesame seed powder to a small bowl and stir in 2 tablespoons of honey. Set aside.

6 In a medium bowl, using a whisk or handheld electric mixer, whip the cream for 2 to 3 minutes, or until soft peaks form.

7 Fold in the black sesame paste. Beat the mixture for about 1 minute more, or until stiff peaks form, and set aside.

8 In a medium sauté pan or skillet over medium heat, heat the remaining 2 tablespoons of honey until it starts to melt and caramelize slightly.

9 Add the banana slices and toss to coat. Cook for 2 to 3 minutes. Add the orange juice to deglaze the pan, stirring with a wooden spoon to loosen any browned bits from the bottom and to coat the bananas. Remove the pan from the heat and set aside.

10 Assemble the napoleons: Spread a small amount of whipped sesame cream on a serving plate and set 1 eggroll wrapper half on top to adhere to the plate. Top the wrapper with caramelized bananas and a dollop of black sesame cream. Place another wrapper half on top and repeat the banana and sesame cream layer. Repeat this process to make five more napoleons.

Vegetarian

Active time:
30 minutes

Total time:
40 minutes

Cooking tip
To separate eggs, you need three tools: clean hands, a flat surface, and two bowls. Crack the egg on the countertop or a cutting board (not the side of the bowl), then open the egg into your cupped hand. Hold the yolk gently and let the white fall through your fingers into one bowl. Place the egg yolk into the other bowl. Repeat as necessary. Wash your hands afterward with soap and hot water.

N[o]tella Lava Cakes
with Strawberries

Serves 4

I saved the best for last: decadent, dark molten lava cake. As far as healthy desserts go, this is certainly an every-once-in-a-while treat, but it's made from whole food ingredients, and it's easier to whip up than you might think.

2 tablespoons unsalted butter, at room temperature

¾ cup all-purpose flour, plus more for dusting

1 pint strawberries, hulled (green tops removed) and thinly sliced, plus more for serving

¼ cup plus 2 tablespoons powdered sugar, divided

Juice of ¼ lemon

1 recipe N[o]tella (page 169)

3 large eggs

2 large egg yolks

½ teaspoon baking powder

¼ teaspoon kosher salt

1 Preheat the oven to 400°F and position a rack in the center of the oven.

2 Coat 4 (4-ounce) ramekins with the butter. Dust each ramekin with flour, knocking out the excess, and refrigerate for 2 to 5 minutes to set.

3 In a small bowl, stir together the strawberries, 2 tablespoons of powdered sugar, and lemon juice. Cover the bowl with plastic wrap and set aside for 20 minutes.

4 In a medium bowl, whisk the N[o]tella, eggs, and egg yolks until smooth and blended.

5 Add the remaining ¾ cup of flour, ¼ cup of powdered sugar, baking powder, and salt. Using a spatula, gently fold to combine the ingredients until smooth. Evenly divide the batter among the chilled ramekins, filling them almost to the top.

6 Bake for exactly 10 minutes so the outsides are set but the insides are still molten. Remove the ramekins from the oven and let cool for at least 3 minutes.

7 Run a knife around the edge of the lava cakes. Place a plate on top of the ramekin and carefully invert the cake onto the plate. Serve with a spoonful of strawberries on the side. Devour immediately.

Sample Menus

After learning to cook all these delicious foods, you'll want to share them. Here are a few sample menus for different occasions to get you started with party planning:

Weeknight Dinner

Salt and Three Pepper Chicken Breasts (page 70)
Spiced Carrots with Pistachios (page 157)
Wild Rice Pilaf (page 164)
5-Ingredient Peanut Butter Pretzel Snaps (page 182)

Dinner with Family or Friends

Blueberry, Rosemary, and Balsamic Pork Loin (page 147)
Peach and Mozzarella Farro Salad (page 50)
Tangerine, Lime, and Mint Spritzer (page 176)
Cherry Chocolate Sherbet (page 183)

Dinner for Two

Prosciutto-Wrapped Steak with Mustard Sauce (page 152)
Grilled Asparagus with Citrus-Herb Butter (page 159)
N[o]tella Lava Cakes with Strawberries (page 190)
Honey-Sriracha Popcorn (if it's also movie night) (page 168)

Measurement Conversions

Volume Equivalents (Liquid)

STANDARD	US STANDARD (OUNCES)	METRIC (APPROXIMATE)
2 TABLESPOONS	1 FL. OZ.	30 ML
¼ CUP	2 FL. OZ.	60 ML
½ CUP	4 FL. OZ.	120 ML
1 CUP	8 FL. OZ.	240 ML
1½ CUPS	12 FL. OZ.	355 ML
2 CUPS OR 1 PINT	16 FL. OZ.	475 ML
4 CUPS OR 1 QUART	32 FL. OZ.	1 L
1 GALLON	128 FL. OZ.	4 L

Oven Temperatures

FAHRENHEIT (F)	CELSIUS (C) (APPROXIMATE)
250°	120°
300°	150°
325°	165°
350°	180°
375°	190°
400°	200°
425°	220°
450°	230°

Volume Equivalents (Dry)

STANDARD	METRIC (APPROXIMATE)
⅛ TEASPOON	0.5 ML
¼ TEASPOON	1 ML
½ TEASPOON	2 ML
¾ TEASPOON	4 ML
1 TEASPOON	5 ML
1 TABLESPOON	15 ML
¼ CUP	59 ML
CUP	79 ML
½ CUP	118 ML
CUP	156 ML
¾ CUP	177 ML
1 CUP	235 ML
2 CUPS OR 1 PINT	475 ML
3 CUPS	700 ML
4 CUPS OR 1 QUART	1 L

Weight Equivalents

STANDARD	METRIC (APPROXIMATE)
½ OUNCE	15 G
1 OUNCE	30 G
2 OUNCES	60 G
4 OUNCES	115 G
8 OUNCES	225 G
12 OUNCES	340 G
16 OUNCES OR 1 POUND	455 G

The Dirty Dozen and the Clean Fifteen™

A nonprofit environmental watchdog organization called Environmental Working Group (EWG) looks at data supplied by the US Department of Agriculture (USDA) and the Food and Drug Administration (FDA) about pesticide residues. Each year it compiles a list of the best and worst pesticide loads found in commercial crops. You can use these lists to decide which fruits and vegetables to buy organic to minimize your exposure to pesticides and which produce is considered safe enough to buy conventionally. This does not mean they are pesticide-free, though, so wash these fruits and vegetables thoroughly. You can find the list online at EWG.org/FoodNews.

Dirty Dozen™

1 strawberries
2 spinach
3 kale
4 nectarines
5 apples
6 grapes
7 peaches
8 cherries
9 pears
10 tomatoes
11 celery
12 potatoes

† Additionally, nearly ¾ of hot pepper samples contained pesticide residues.

Clean Fifteen™

1 avocados
2 sweet corn*
3 pineapples
4 sweet peas (frozen)
5 onions
6 papayas*
7 eggplants
8 asparagus
9 kiwis
10 cabbages
11 cauliflower
12 cantaloupes
13 broccoli
14 mushrooms
15 honeydew melons

* A small amount of sweet corn, papaya, and summer squash sold in the United States is produced from genetically modified seeds. Buy organic varieties of these crops if you want to avoid genetically modified produce.

Resources

The following resources provide more information on healthy eating and cooking, seasonal eating and shopping, and more.

Culinary Institute of America. *Techniques of Healthy Cooking*. Hoboken: Wiley, 2013.

FoodPrint. "Seasonal Food Guide." Accessed July 18, 2019. www.seasonal foodguide.org.

Harvard Health Publishing. "Healthy Eating." Accessed July 18, 2019. www.health .harvard.edu/topics/healthy-eating.

Magee, Elaine. "The Whole Foods Diet." WebMD. Accessed July 18, 2019. www.webmd.com/food-recipes/features/the-whole-foods-diet#1.

PBS. *Well Fed: Nourishing Our Children for a Lifetime*. Accessed July 18, 2019. www.pbs.org/video/health-documentaries-well-fed-nourishing-our-children -lifetime.

Pollan, Michael. *The Omnivore's Dilemma*. New York: Penguin, 2006.

Utter, Jennifer, Nicole Larson, Melissa N. Laska, Megan Winkler, and Dianne Neumark-Sztainer. "Self-Perceived Cooking Skills in Emerging Adulthood Predict Better Dietary Behaviors And Intake 10 Years Later: A Longitudinal Study." *Journal of Nutrition Education and Behavior* 50, no. 5 (May 2018): 494–500. doi:10.1016/j.jneb.2018.01.021.

Woodruff, Sarah J., and Ashley R. Kirby. "The Associations Among Family Meal Frequency, Food Preparation Frequency, Self-Efficacy for Cooking, and Food Preparation Techniques in Children and Adolescents." *Journal of Nutrition Education and Behavior* 45, no. 4 (July-August 2013): 296–303. doi:10.1016/ j.jneb.2012.11.006.

Index

Acknowledgments

The creation of this book would not have been possible without a plethora of incredible people.

Thanks, first and foremost, to my amazing team at Callisto Media—my acquisitions editor, Vanessa Putt; my editor, Eliza Kirby; my developmental editor, Mary Cassells; and my design and marketing teams. Your comments, critiques, and guidance were invaluable throughout this entire process. Without your collaboration, I would never have written a cookbook of this scale and caliber.

Thanks also to my family near and far—especially my recipe testers: my mother, Deborah; my brother, Benjamin; my grandmother, Madeline; and my great-aunt, Susan. Thank you for lending me your kitchens, your feedback, and your stomachs. I love you all very dearly, and I look forward to speaking to, seeing, and feeding you as soon as possible. Another special thanks to Mary Clarke for the incredible vegetable stew recipe; it's an honor to include it in this book.

Next, I must acknowledge my friends, coworkers, cheerleaders, and mentors—in my two homes, Orlando and Durham, and elsewhere. Thank you for believing in me and supporting my gastronomic pursuits. Your awesomeness needs no explanation, and I'm truly privileged to bring my food into our ongoing adventures and endeavors. Here's to many more meals and memories together.

And, lastly, a brief thank you to all the chefs, restaurants, and recipes I've had the pleasure to encounter over my eight years and counting in the kitchen. Your work inspires me to keep cooking. The paths you've forged have helped me forge my own.

I wish you all the best, and I can only fathom our great future ahead.

About the Author

Noah Michaud has honed his cooking skills since the age of 12. Until September 2017, he kept up a blog, *The Teen Gourmet*. Since then, he has posted on his second project, *The Collegiate Connoisseur*. Noah hails from Orlando, Florida, where he has been involved in the local food scene and has had his recipes featured in the *Orlando Sentinel*.

When he's not in the kitchen, Noah studies as a junior at Duke University in Durham, North Carolina, where he has also studied food academically and hosted a cooking demo in the university's Chef's Kitchen. He is beyond excited to have written this book and hopes you enjoy it!

CPSIA information can be obtained
at www.ICGtesting.com
Printed in the USA
LVHW071913281019
635583LV00014B/291/P